Path of Valor:
A Marine's Story

by

George Derryberry

Roy Stewart
805 N Second St
Amite, La 70422

TABLE OF CONTENTS

INTRODUCTION

by

Lieutenant General Lawrence F. Snowden,
USMC (Retired)

As a young Marine officer in my twenties, I served in the Twenty-Third Marine Regiment both before and after it formed the nucleus of the new Fourth Marine Division at Camp Pendleton, California, in August of 1943. As such, I had the honor and privilege of commanding Marines in infantry companies of the Twenty-Third Marines as we fought the Japanese in the central Pacific. With the sea at our backs, and a well-trained, tenacious enemy determined to resist to the death before us, Marines in our regiment and others captured and secured at great cost the islands of Roi-Namur, Saipan, Tinian, and Iwo Jima within a period of thirteen months. We survivors of these battles were recovering, reorganizing, and training to invade the home islands of Japan when the war ended.

From this perspective, I read *Path of Valor: A Marine's Story*. This book, the product of author George Derryberry's monumental research of official records and operation reports, and interviews with Marine veterans of the campaign with some of whom I served, is a powerful and unflinching account of the experiences of young Marines and their buddies, from enlistment and boot camp, through training and embarkation with the Twenty-Third Marines as part of the Fleet Marine Force Pacific, and their experiences in combat from Roi-Namur to Iwo Jima. The book is a fine piece of work, a very good read, and well-deserving of its place among the growing collection of books about United States Marines who served in World War II.

Lawrence F. Snowden

FOREWORD

Marine Corps Base Camp Lejeune sprawls over 246 square miles of flat, pine forested coastal plain on North Carolina's eastern shore where the New River enters the Atlantic Ocean. The base, renamed from "New River" for General John Lejeune after his death in 1942, has changed little since the early 1960s when my good friend, Marine Lance Corporal Delmar Lee Reynolds, served there with the Second Marine Division's Shore Party Battalion.

During those Cold War years of uneasy peace, the duties of Second Division Marines fluctuated among armed deployments to the Caribbean and Mediterranean, rigorous field and weapons training, and occasional tedious work details. On one such work detail in September of 1962, Lee and others in his unit were assigned to destroy unserviceable "782 gear," consisting of packs, canteens, and web gear. While carrying an armload of damaged canteens to a truck for delivery to a crusher, Lee glanced down and noticed a peculiar scarred pattern on one canteen. He loaded all of the canteens into the truck, except this one. Then, turning the well-worn 1944 canteen about in the early autumn sunlight, he was able to make out several words that had been etched with a sharp object into its surface:

> SURIBACHI TAKEN I'M
> ON IT. KILLED 3 JAPS
> IWO JIMA ROUF GO
> MOVING ON TO CAVES
> IF I DON'T MAKE IT
> BACK TELL BETTY
> H. C. Ayres
> 23rd Marines
> 2/23/1945

The entire lot of canteens and other unserviceable equipment was ordered destroyed, and thus abandoned. Lee completed his assigned duties on the work detail, but kept the canteen that bore the hand-etched message.

Only seventeen years had passed since the Allied victory over Japan in World War II. Many surviving veterans of the Pacific campaign remained on active duty in Marine Corps units, including the Second Division. These non-commissioned officers occasionally displayed their Rising Sun battle flags, captured Japanese weapons, and other memorabilia to each other and to the new breed of younger enlisted Marines such as Lee, with whom they served and whom they led. On such occasions, Lee showed the 1944 canteen with its inscribed message to these Marines, but the "salty" Pacific veterans viewed it only as a mildly interesting relic, and as less exotic than their own battlefield trophies. Few of the older veterans even troubled to inspect the faintly scratched message on the canteen's surface.

Lee, however, was struck by the terse, evocative message from Iwo Jima. The few etched lines spoke of the Marine's proximity to Mount Suribachi on the day it fell, grimly tallied his own engagements with the enemy four days after the landing on February 19, 1945, and revealed a stoic awareness of what he would face upon resuming the advance against the heavily defended and interconnected Japanese tunnels, caves, and pillboxes to the north. His poignant closing revealed a measure of affection and concern for a lady who had to have been special to him.

Marines on active duty in the early sixties, as now, had little time or opportunity for such pursuits as researching the fate of World War II veterans. To make matters worse, the Internet would not appear for decades, and tools and resources available for such inquiries were comparatively crude. Lee therefore safeguarded the canteen, hoping that someday he might be able to learn more about this Marine and his message from Iwo Jima. Perhaps H. C. Ayres had returned alive and well from World War II. Perhaps he had returned to Betty's welcoming arms. Perhaps the aging veteran, or Betty, or both of them survived and would be excited and pleased to see this memento from their dramatic past.

These intriguing possibilities lingered and beckoned for years. Eventually, the effects of injuries that Lee had received in an accident seriously hampered any research. Wishing to spare the canteen a second consignment to oblivion, and stating to me that, "A Marine carried this canteen, and another Marine should have it," Lee entrusted this relic from the Marine Corps' most violent and costly battle to my care. In return, I made two silent and unsolicited promises: That I would treat the Marine's canteen with the respect it deserved, and that I would do my best to search out all I could about the man who carried the canteen ashore on Iwo Jima and paused during the bitter fighting to inscribe his haunting message.

This book presents the results of that long search. It tells the story of a young American who volunteered to serve his country with the "first to fight" in a time of immense danger, and who became a hero by the definition that has resonated most strongly with many Marine veterans, including two of the surviving flag-raisers in Joe Rosenthal's famous Mount Suribachi photograph. Such men, when hailed as heroes, replied in quiet protest that the real heroes were the ones who never came back.

I hope and intend that my work and words honor the young Marine whose message languished for years, and also the tens of thousands of his comrades in arms who risked and often gave their lives in the brutal and difficult Pacific island campaign. Landing on the island of Guadalcanal in the Solomon Islands in America's first land offensive of World War II, the First Marine Division, despite the Allied "Europe first" strategy, meager rations and supplies, and the absence of adequate or consistent naval gunfire and fleet air support, defeated the

Japanese in a grueling jungle campaign, ending their uninterrupted string of victories in Asia and the Pacific. Advancing thousands of miles further in an island-hopping campaign through the southwest and central Pacific, Marines attacked and secured the Japanese-held northern Solomons, the Gilberts, Marshalls, Marianas, Pelelui in the Palaus, Iwo Jima in the Volcano Islands, and Okinawa in the Ryukyus. Marines in six separate divisions attacked and seized by frontal amphibious assault the most devilishly conceived positions and tenaciously defended terrain in the history of modern warfare.

By August of 1945, they had crossed the Pacific and stood poised on Japan's doorstep. Despite suffering horrific casualties in numbers that stirred protests by many homebound beneficiaries of their efforts, these Marines never faltered or entertained any thought of the possibility of defeat. They had no "exit strategy." Their strategy was to accomplish their missions or die trying. Their end game was to win by killing the enemy. They fought in harsh conditions for as hard and as long as necessary to achieve a complete American victory over a skilled and implacable enemy whose commanders ordered death and even suicide rather than surrender. The legendary courage and determination of these leathernecks has inspired, and will continue to inspire, later generations of Marines, including this writer.

In the decades following 1945, innumerable well-researched and published accounts have described every element of the Pacific campaign from Pearl Harbor through Hiroshima and Nagasaki. This book will not attempt to recycle these excellent studies of the war against Japan. Instead, it will focus primarily on the life and experiences of Harris C. Ayres, Jr., and the comrades who served closely with him in Company M, and later Company I of the Third Battalion, Twenty-Third Marines, Fourth Marine Division before and during the four major Pacific invasions in which the division fought from February of 1944 through March of 1945. Ayres' Fourth Division earned two Presidential Unit Citations and a plethora of individual battle decorations during a period of thirteen months of intense combat in the central Pacific.

The praiseworthy achievements of other Marines, other units, and other armed service branches are described briefly to provide context. This focus is not intended, and should not be construed, as indifference to the accomplishments of those units or their service members. Indeed, as more of these veterans pass on from us each day, their service and sacrifice should never be forgotten by the citizens of this nation whose freedom they fought, suffered, and died to preserve.

CHAPTER 1

IN THE BEGINNING

In the years between the armistice ending World War I and the 1929 market crash propelling the United States into the Great Depression, a generation of American boys began their lives in innocence, unaware of the approach of another far more cataclysmic event that would impact every inhabited continent and decimate many of the earth's major populations. The lives and destinies of this generation of American boys, or those who were blessed with sound minds and bodies, would be deeply influenced, if not consumed by a coming global war.

These future Marines, sailors, soldiers, and aviators were born and raised in great cities, small towns, and on farms and ranches throughout the United States. This story begins in Susquehanna County, part of the "northern tier" of northeastern Pennsylvania, just below the New York state line. This pleasant and scenic county is blessed with green hills and valleys, clear lakes and streams, and abundant crops, timber, and wildlife. Those who are born there tend to stay there. The county's seat, and in many ways its crown jewel, is the Borough of Montrose. There, on September 1, 1923, a son was born to Harris Carpenter Ayres, a taciturn twenty-two year old automobile mechanic, and Nina, his wife of three years. Harris and Nina named their son Harris Carpenter Ayres, Jr. after his father. He would be their only child.

Young Harris and his parents made their home in a sturdy frame house on Monument Square near the town center of Montrose. Harris, Sr.'s place of business, Ayres' Garage, was located at seventeen Chestnut Street, less than a block from the family's home. As a grade-schooler, Harris, Jr. soon acquired the nickname "Ayresie" from family and friends. On week days, he walked across the grassy town square or "green," with its monument to soldiers who fought for the Union in the Civil War, to attend a three-story brick schoolhouse on Lake Avenue, where students in grades one through twelve were taught.

As Ayresie grew into his high school years, a lively and good-natured personality emerged and developed. In this respect, Ayresie was different from his stolid father. By the time Ayresie had entered Montrose High School, his penchant for rambunctious and good-natured hijinks was apparent to all who knew him. His average academic performance was balanced by his popularity, by his eagerness to take the lead, and by his willingness to undertake such extracurricular activities as the Hi Y Club and yearbook staff.

No youngster's life is perfectly idyllic, and Ayresie's early years were no exception. Unfortunately, from the time Ayresie was an eighth grader there were signs of serious friction between his father and mother. Despite hard economic times during the Great Depression, the couple's trouble did not seem to be financial. Ayres' Garage was a successful business, which continued to survive, if not thrive, during the 1930s and 1940s. Nevertheless, the relationship between Harris and Nina clearly was suffering, and marked by heated arguments and perhaps worse. Without siblings at home, Ayresie had no choice but to witness and experience this heartbreaking conflict alone.

Ayresie's family owned a small cottage which sat on the shore of Forest Lake eight miles outside Montrose. The family spent many weekends there, and longer periods during the temperate Pennsylvania summers. Ayresie and his friends often gathered to swim and socialize at Forest Lake. The 185-acre lakeside farm of Arthur and Velma Potts was nearby, where the couple lived with their three children, brothers Delbert and Norval and older sister Elizabeth. The Potts family was well acquainted with Harris and Nina Ayres through the proximity of the Ayres' cottage to their farm, and through Arthur Potts' occasional need for the services of the skilled garageman. Ayresie thus came to know Arthur and Velma Potts and their three children. As he grew in strength and experience, he enthusiastically tackled chores for Arthur Potts, and eventually was able to assist him with any farm task.

By age fourteen, Ayresie regularly worked on weekends for Arthur and daily during the summer months. To reach the farm from his home in Montrose, Ayresie pedaled his single speed bicycle over an eight-mile road that wound through the wooded hills and pastures of rural Susquehanna County.

At five feet nine inches, Ayresie was not particularly tall. However, the steady farm work he came to love soon produced a stout, muscular physique and an innate toughness. Following one difficult day working hay in the loft of the Potts' barn, Ayresie appeared for supper in the kitchen of the farmhouse. He was fatigued, and completely oblivious to a copious amount of dried blood that was plainly visible on his head and neck. Velma Potts, startled and concerned, cried out, "Why, Harris, what on Earth happened to you?" Ayresie calmly replied that an exposed roofing nail in the barn had pierced his scalp while he was working in the loft. Ignoring the bleeding wound, he continued his task throughout the entire afternoon until suppertime. Velma cleaned and bandaged the injury, scolding Ayresie for neglecting it. She could not have known how well his toughness and stoicism would serve him in the years to come.

Immediately following the completion of his junior year at Montrose High School, Ayresie moved from the Ayres home in Montrose to the Potts farmhouse on a full-time basis. This move eliminated the difficult bicycle ride to and from the farm. Whether or not intended, his relocation also reduced his exposure to the quarrels of his parents.

In this difficult time, Ayresie essentially became a surrogate member of this hard-working, devoutly Christian family. He was gently encouraged to attend church with the family, was given his own separate bedroom in the farmhouse, and was immediately accepted into the household, not only by Arthur and Velma, but also by their three children. Ayresie was "like a brother" to Delbert Potts, who was then only eight years old. Ayresie worked hard with Arthur when there was work to be done and enjoyed energetic horseplay with his near-siblings at other times. Arthur and Velma and their three children came to love Ayresie as if he were their own son and brother.

Ayresie's life was not all work and spirited play with the Potts siblings and his high school chums. The Ayres' cottage was one of many on the shores of Forest Lake. The owners of another lakeside cottage regularly invited their comely young granddaughter, Harriette Whitney Weston of Endicott, New York, to spend the summer months with them.

This vibrant, young woman quickly caught Ayresie's eye, and he wasted no time approaching the pert sophomore. The couple soon developed a strong, mutual attraction, and their relationship grew more serious as they passed the summer of 1940 in the pleasant lakeside setting. Within weeks, Ayresie and Harriette became "steadies" who were strongly devoted to each other. Thirty-five miles separated Montrose and Endicott, but the couple overcame this challenge during the school year whenever opportunities arose, and wasted no time renewing and strengthening their bond during the summer of 1941 at Forest Lake.

Ayresie's warm acceptance into the Potts family, their quiet nurturing of his spirituality, his work with Arthur, his love for the surrounding countryside, and the strong emotional bond he shared with his sweetheart all provided emotional support, which helped him to cope with the pain of his parents' deteriorating relationship.

At the beginning of his senior year at Montrose High School in September of 1940, Ayresie's academic achievements remained no better than average. In contrast, his burgeoning confidence, enthusiasm, and natural leadership qualities were at an all-time high. He had continued to develop and flourish physically under the regimen of work at the Potts farm and during his many opportunities to hike, hunt, and fish in the surrounding woods and streams.

As he matured, Ayresie began to form a plan for his life. He envisioned owning his own small farm somewhere near the Potts spread in Susquehanna County and a lifetime with his sweetheart and their eventual children. These dreams and ambitions formed and grew, despite the alarming Nazi victories in Europe, the perilous struggles of Great Britain under the Nazi blitz, and the ominous advances of Japanese forces in China and elsewhere in Asia. Susquehanna County and America in general remained passive, and stubbornly continued to yearn for isolation from these developments far across the broad Atlantic and Pacific Oceans.

After his high school graduation in early June of 1941, Ayresie continued to enjoy the summer months at Forest Lake with the Potts family and Harriette. As summer turned to fall, Ayresie continued to live and work at the Potts farm, saving as much of his earnings as possible for the future. Harriette returned to Endicott for her senior high school year, following the summer spent at Forest Lake.

Harris at Forest Lake, Summer, 1941

*Harriette Weston outside her family's cottage
at Forest Lake, Summer, 1941*

On Sunday, December 7, 1941, all illusions of America's continued isolation from the world's growing conflicts were shattered. The entire Potts family was relaxing in their living room, listening to the radio. Following the usual Sunday dinner, Ayresie lay dozing on the living room sofa with his head cradled in Velma Potts' lap. Suddenly, at about 2:30 p.m., the first reports of the Pearl Harbor sneak attack were broadcast. As the family listened in shock to the emerging details of Japanese perfidy and the death and destruction at Pearl Harbor, Ayresie rose, glowering from the couch. "We have to do something about this."

Ayresie's fury at the Japanese was shared by the entire nation. Young men flocked to recruiting stations en masse, volunteering to fight the hated Japanese and avenge the servicemen and civilians killed at Pearl Harbor. Thousands who were determined to serve with the "toughest" or "first to fight" sought to volunteer for service in the United States Marine Corps. This influx of volunteers virtually swamped Marine Corps recruiting and training facilities. Ayresie and others yearning to strike back at the "Japs" had weeks or even months to put their affairs in order. Ayresie gave his trusty hunting rifle to Norval Potts. He arranged for Arthur Potts to board and use his dearly bought farm horse whenever needed.

On August 10, 1942, Ayresie bade farewell to Harriette, the Potts family, and his own parents, and reported to the Marine Corps recruiting station in Binghamton, New York. There, he simultaneously enlisted with a group of thirteen other young men from southern New York and northern Pennsylvania. Photographs of these recruits, resplendent in a pre-cut and adjustable version of the Marine Corps iconic dress blue uniform designed for this specific purpose, appeared with a patriotic article in the Binghamton newspaper.

Ayresie, like thousands of other volunteers, had, without hesitation, stepped forward to "do something" about the Japanese aggression against his country for the duration of the emergency.

CHAPTER 2

METAMORPHOSIS: THE MARINE

For over a century, US Marine Corps "boot camp" has been a traditional rite of passage that is both initiation into an elite warrior society and strenuous training for armed conflicts. The ordeal is shared and remembered by every Marine, young and old. From beginning to end, the experience is unique among the training programs of all military organizations.

Uniqueness is apparent at the very inception of the process, during recruiting. The Marine Corps never has attempted to lure enlistees with such blandishments as technical preparation for a civilian career, preferred military duty assignments, or guaranteed occupational specialties. The Marine Corps does not hold itself out as a means to a civilian end. Its basic need is for disciplined and skilled riflemen. The Marine Corps' offer to any who would join its ranks is simple, and its appeal is deliberately targeted at those who aspire to become part of an elite, highly motivated, warrior class: Join us, and you may make the grade. If you do, you will serve with the best, and you will be the best. The promise is not the lesser assurance that you will be "the best that you can be." The Corps' promise to a recruit who passes its difficult requirements is that he will be the best, period. This esprit de corps is reflected by the rousing final stanza of the "Marines' Hymn," and each recruit must learn every verse by heart:

If the Army and the Navy ever look on Heaven's scenes,

They will find the streets are guarded by United States Marines!

Acceptance of this challenge through voluntary enlistment, however laudable, does not elevate the status of the recruit; the opposite is true. These neophytes are by no means full-fledged Marines, and this point is early and strongly made. "Boots" who unwisely describe themselves as Marines while in recruit training invariably receive an immediate and hostile rebuke or worse from their drill instructor or "DI," accompanied by eloquent profanity, and often some imaginative form of group punishment. The lesson is quickly learned. No person who has not survived the crucible of boot camp may describe himself as a Marine. Until the recruit has successfully completed each and every physical, intellectual, and military training requirement of basic training and has passed in review with his platoon at his graduation ceremony, he is accustomed to his drill instructor's use of colorful, obscene appellations, each of which leaves no doubt that he faces a continuing ordeal before he may claim the title of United States Marine.

The verbal and physical abuse to which Marine recruits traditionally have been exposed has prompted decades of criticism from many quarters. Such criticism ignores the Marine Corps' uncomplicated view of its initial training task, which is to instill discipline. The Marine Corps intends to destroy the civilian's cautious and analytical approach to danger, and to construct in its place the instinct to obey orders promptly and without question, and to accomplish all assigned missions no matter the consequences. Marines are trained to "do or die" immediately and without question.

The Marine Corps' early emphasis on marching and close order drill also has been questioned from time to time. This training component is not intended solely to prepare Marines for ceremonial duties, however important they are to Marine Corps tradition. All recruits, including the majority who are destined for field or combat assignments, undergo this repetitive drill for hours on end and in all weathers. The truth is that close order drill has, for decades if not for centuries, instilled discipline and teamwork, and has cultivated the conditioned response of instant obedience to orders of a superior officer or NCO. The lesson and response are not complicated. Listen up, Marine, and obey quickly.

The Corps' employment of stress, and its fundamental approach to training in general were not developed as a product of humanistic philosophy or academic debate. The reciprocal objectives of the Marine Corps and its recruits are to train and be trained as thoroughly and effectively as possible to win what may be the most challenging of all armed conflicts. Developing in recruits the instinct to follow orders, employ skills, and achieve objectives while under severe emotional stress unquestionably has contributed to the achievement of this objective.

World War II amphibious landings on the Pacific islands, for which Harris Ayres and hundreds of thousands of others like him were trained, were made against a well-prepared and fanatical enemy, eager to kill our attacking forces by the use of every type of weapon and tactic imaginable. At critical points in every assault, especially in its early stages when invading troops were at their most vulnerable, these battles became confused, disorienting maelstroms. In such situations, carefully rehearsed plans, landing sites, and unit cohesion all were altered if not obliterated. Time and again under these conditions, small "ad hoc" units, formed by both experienced and inexperienced but well trained Marines, were confronted by devastating artillery and automatic weapons fire, unit disruption, and the sight of their killed or mutilated comrades. Despite these horrors, which can barely be imagined by those who have not shared them and survived the experience, individual Marines in small groups continued to advance by fire and maneuver to close with and kill the enemy. Marine veterans of the Pacific invasions acknowledge that their training in boot camp and the bonds created by that shared challenge helped enable them to persevere where others may have faltered and failed.

On August 10, 1942, as the First Marine Division fought in their fourth day of battle on Guadalcanal, Harris and other area volunteers who had enlisted with him in Binghamton, New York, were examined in Syracuse, New York and cleared medically for training. They immediately boarded a passenger train bound for Parris Island, South Carolina, where they would commence the transformation from farm hands, factory workers, students, or the unemployed to skilled warriors and from civilian individuals to United States Marines.

Upon their arrival, Harris and his mates were abruptly met by livid and screaming drill instructors, wearing pressed and perfectly fitting khakis, gleaming spit-shined shoes, and broad-brimmed "Smokey the Bear" campaign caps. These seasoned and impressive non-commissioned officers derided the recruits' very legitimacy, announced that they now occupied the lowest level of human existence, and questioned their fitness to be present. Barking instructions in voices that approached the threshold of pain, they quickly formed Harris and seventy-one other disoriented recruits into Recruit Platoon 621 and thrust them into a frenzied flurry of activity.

Each recruit was issued sage green field uniforms called "dungarees," consisting of cotton herringbone trousers and shirt-type jackets with the eagle, globe, and anchor symbol stenciled on the left breast pocket. Each received rough-side-out, ankle-high field shoes called "boondockers," canvas leggings, caps, helmets, packs, canteens, and other field equipment. All were quickly shorn of individual hair styles by unsympathetic barbers who reduced their variety of scalp adornments to stubble within seconds.

The platoon was then marched in a rough semblance of military formation to "chow," where they were told they could take all they wanted, but warned that woe would betide those who failed to eat all they took. After marching from the mess hall, they were ordered to clean and organize their barracks, all the while being loudly chastised and excoriated. The process of transformation, made even more urgent by the demands of wartime, had begun.

The frantically completed intake tasks soon were followed by instruction in proper platoon formation, basic facing movements, and early stages of close order drill. Harris and his companions literally relearned how to stand—at attention, completely immobile, with backs straight, feet outward at a forty-five degree angle, thumbs along trouser seams, and eyes fixed in a steady, unfocused gaze forward, without daring to meet the eyes of their DI or any inspecting officer.

Next came marching in platoon formation, eventually in proper step and alignment, and responding as one to the commands of their DIs –"Column right…march! Left flank… march!" These commands were loudly given in a strange dialect, spoken only by members of the elite cadre of Marine drill instructors. Their language eliminated most consonants, stretched vowels to their limits of malleability, and otherwise altered the pronunciation of ordinary English words. At the command "Left flank…march!" each recruit in Platoon 621 was to take one more step with his right foot, pivot ninety degrees to the left, and step out in the new direction with the left foot. In DI Speak, this command rang out in some variation of "Y'lelf 'haaank…hunh!" Proper march cadence might be a near-musical rendition of "left, right, left," which might be heard as "h'lelf, 'ight, h'lelf." Harris and his platoon soon came to understand this language, which they easily distinguished from the similarly altered commands of other DIs to their own platoons marching nearby. Within days, Platoon 621 was marching in step, their DI's cadence reinforced by the rhythmic strike of their boondocker heels against the "parade deck."

Harris and his mates were not marching aboard some spacious naval vessel. The recruits, future soldiers of the sea, were learning the Corps' own nautical language, shared with their senior but rival service, the United States Navy. The civilian floor, and even the ground outside, became the "deck." All ceilings, walls, and doors were, respectively, "overheads, bulkheads, and hatches." The bathroom was the "head;" stairways became "ladders;" a bunk was a "rack." A drinking fountain became a "scuttlebutt;" the medical clinic the "sick bay;" a helmet or garrison cap a "cover;" and a jail or prison the "brig."

As training progressed, Recruit Platoon 621's DIs continued to appear suddenly from unseen vantage points to castigate and ultimately correct all imperfections in personal hygiene, the appearance of uniforms, execution of commands in close order drill, use of proper parlance, or carefully cleaning and organizing the platoon's squad bay and head until they were spotless and "squared away." Recruits were taught to perform the "Marine Corps way." Especially severe was any substandard performance in handling and proper care of weapons, specifically the 30.06 caliber, bolt-action 1903 Springfield rifle issued to Harris' platoon in its second week of training.

Most recruits soon adapted to strict requirements for impeccable barracks, uniforms, and equipment, but few were prepared for the even more stringent Marine Corps standards for the care, cleaning, and use of individual weapons. Before Harris was allowed the privilege of firing his Springfield rifle, he, like every other member of Platoon 621, was required to memorize its serial number, its full nomenclature, and its functions. Each recruit in Platoon 621 was taught to quickly field-strip, clean, and reassemble his rifle, and to prepare it perfectly for painstaking inspections by the platoon's DIs or platoon commander.

DIs' harassment and hectoring were not ends in themselves. Parris Island has always had as its objective the production of disciplined and skilled Marines, regarded by most as the most motivated, disciplined, and capable warriors on Earth. Thus, the drill instructors' implacable insistence upon exactness of response to orders and absolute discipline coincided with intense, thorough training in individual combat skills. Harris and others in his platoon were thoroughly instructed and required to practice to exhaustion their basic marksmanship skills, and techniques of hand to hand combat. Harris' nineteenth birthday was spent learning and practicing with the other recruits in Platoon 621 the art of killing with the long-bladed bayonet fixed to their Springfield rifles.

As the Marine Corps expanded quickly to meet the demands of the Pacific island-hopping campaign, already well underway as Marines fought toward victory in the Solomon Islands, Harris and his platoon struggled through the rigors of Parris Island. During 1942 and for months and years thereafter, thousands of recruits converged upon the Marine Corps' two recruit depots at Parris Island and San Diego, California. To meet this challenge, the Marine Corps compressed its boot camp training schedule from twelve to eight weeks. However, no element of training was omitted or short-changed. Training days normally commenced with reveille no later than 4:30 a.m. or "0430," and concluded with taps no earlier than 10:00 p.m. or "2200."

Platoon 621's critical forming, processing, and fundamental indoctrination in Marine Corps traditions and discipline, drill, and basic training in hand to hand combat and bayonet fighting were all accomplished within four weeks at Parris Island. Thereafter, following a final inspection and battalion parade, Platoon 621 and other recruit platoons in the same training cycle packed their gear and equipment and travelled by troop train 350 miles northward to the recently constructed Marine Corps Base at Camp Lejeune, North Carolina. The balance of Harris' recruit training would occur in the forests and on the beaches and weapons ranges of this immense, new base.

At Camp Lejeune, a subtle shift in the approach to basic training occurred. The fundamentals of strict discipline, drill, the manual of arms, and familiarity with hand to hand combat and infantry weapons had been instilled at Parris Island. Now, it was time to hone the motivated and newly disciplined recruits into full-fledged Marines, not only eager but also fully competent to defeat the similarly motivated and disciplined perpetrators of the Greater East Asia Co-Prosperity Sphere. At Camp Lejeune, the recruits would take their rudimentary combat skills to a higher level.

An immediate priority was individual rifle marksmanship. A traditional Marine Corps adage holds that "every Marine is a rifleman," whether officer or enlisted, infantryman, artilleryman, tanker, cook, or clerk. Shortly after their arrival and assignment to hastily erected shelters, Harris and his platoon were issued rifle score books, and were marched several miles to New River's rifle range where they would consummate their intimate relationship with the 1903 Springfield rifle.

As an experienced hunter, Harris held an advantage over most of the other young men in Platoon 621. However, even his self-taught skills were to be remolded into techniques proven by decades of Marine marksmanship. For hours, Platoon 621 practiced steadying their weapons with the rifle's leather sling in four separate positions: Standing or "off hand," sitting, kneeling, and prone. All platoon members became accustomed to holding precisely correct sight alignment and "picture," and steadily increasing pressure on the rifle's trigger to achieve a "surprise shot," overcoming the uninitiated shooter's natural instinct to anticipate, flinch, and miss the target. These skills were practiced for hours in a "snapping in" ritual, which exactly duplicated live firing in all respects, save for the absence of live ammunition. An unanticipated "snap" of the firing pin on an empty chamber while the rifle was held on target with proper sight picture and alignment signaled a successful shot.

Soon, Harris and his platoon were issued 30.06 caliber ammunition and began live firing from distances of 200, 300, and 500 yards. On the firing range, no screaming drill instructors harassed the recruits. At this critical stage of training, experienced range instructors quietly observed, assisted, and encouraged each "shooter," providing corrections where needed. To qualify, every recruit would be required to score at least 190 out of a possible 250 points while shooting for record.

Days of preparatory firing accustomed the shooters to the time-honored range routine. "Lock and load. Is the line ready? The line is ready. All ready on the right…all ready on the left? All ready on the firing line. Stand by." As the row of shooters waited, poised in the designated firing position with their loaded rifles, a long row of targets simultaneously appeared in the air from the "butts" down range, lifted in unison by other shooters who had completed or not yet commenced firing. In "slow fire" from certain positions and distances, ten rounds were fired with no time limit. During "rapid fire," recruits fired ten shots within a specific firing interval, quickly reloading their Springfields with another five-round clip after firing the first five. The fusillade of rapid fire, combined with random slow firing, soon accustomed the shooters to the loud reports of rifles fired nearby, which would distract the uninitiated or untrained.

Near the end of their basic training, Platoon 621 fired for record. Harris was the only member of Platoon 621 who fired "expert," the highest of three qualifying grades, entitling him to an additional five dollars per month in pay, an increase of roughly 25 percent. He also was entitled to wear the coveted expert's medal, a silver laurel wreath, over the left breast of his newly issued dark green Kersey wool winter service uniform.

At the conclusion of eight difficult and demanding weeks of boot camp, including all-important qualification with the Springfield rifle, recruit training was completed. Harris had made the grade and had earned the coveted title of United States Marine—Private Harris C. Ayres, Jr., Service Number 428622, United States Marine Corps Reserve.

At this point, Platoon 621 and all other platoons of graduating recruits simply ceased to exist. Most of their members would now be assigned to combat units in the Fleet Marine Force.

CHAPTER 3

MIKE COMPANY

Harris and the other Marines graduating from Recruit Platoon 621 faced a variety of potential duty assignments as they prepared to enter the Fleet Marine Force. The greater number of them would become riflemen assigned to rifle companies in the infantry regiments of the Marine Corps. Some would become cannoneers and mortarmen, tankers, flame thrower men, combat engineers, or join the crews of amphibious assault craft. Others would be assigned to such logistical support units as supply, shore party, and motor transport. These Marines would be responsible for maintaining an uninterrupted flow of rations, ammunition, and medical supplies—the "beans, bullets, and band aids" vital to combat troops on the battlefield.

Harris, a compact and powerful man, and a crack shot who qualified as an expert rifleman at boot camp, fit the classic mold for a machine gunner. He was immediately assigned to M Company or "Mike" Company, the machine gun company of the newly formed Twenty-Third Marine Regiment, called the "Twenty-Third Marines," at Camp Lejeune.

The Marines assigned to Mike Company immediately commenced an intense and demanding training schedule to achieve full expertise in maintaining, carrying, positioning, and firing the Browning M1917 A2 water-cooled machine gun. This formidable crew-served weapon, which had seen service in World War I, weighed almost one hundred pounds when mounted on its fifty-pound steel tripod. It was capable of firing 450 rounds per minute of belted 30.06 ammunition through its water-cooled, jacketed barrel at a nominal effective range of up to 2,500 yards.

The pace of training in Mike Company rivaled and occasionally exceeded that of boot camp. However, the hectoring the men had received from their drill instructors was supplanted by calmer and less distracting methods. No longer "boots," these Marines were hurriedly but thoroughly learning their deadly craft. The consensus of the Mike Company Marines, as expressed by one Marine writing home to his family, was that "they treat us like men here."

Living in the close quarters of his twenty-man, oil-heated hut with other machine gunners in Company M, Third Battalion, Twenty-Third Marines, or "M Company, 3-23," Harris formed strong friendships with other Marines.

Robert W. Avery, a handsome "recruiting poster" Marine from Newark Valley, New York, left high school after his junior year to help support his family by working in a shoe factory. He had enlisted with Harris on August 10, 1942 in Binghamton, New York, and had fired "sharpshooter," the level immediately below Ayresie's "expert," with the Springfield rifle at Camp Lejeune. Bob Avery, who qualified second only to Harris with the rifle, was assigned to Mike Company, and the two young Marines quickly formed a close and strong friendship.

Ayresie, Robert Avery, and fellow M Company Marine Harper engage in some spirited horseplay outside their hut at Camp Lejeune, late fall, 1942.

Tom Savery, a strapping, three-sport athlete from Valley Stream on New York's Long Island, already had experienced a unique opportunity to handle and fire the Browning heavy machine gun while a student at Valley Stream High School. He had volunteered for the Civilian Military Training Corps at Fort Dix, New Jersey, and had planned to follow the example of his older brothers who joined the US Army. Tom's plans changed when a respected friend who served in the Marine Corps came home on leave, resplendent in his dress blue uniform. Tom, like thousands of other young men, was so impressed with his friend's obvious pride and military bearing that he changed his plans, and the local Marine Corps recruiter's quota was reduced by one. Upon his graduation from boot camp, Tom's assembled formation was asked by an officer if any man had previous experience with machine guns. Alone among his platoon mates, Tom raised his hand.

William H. Rutkowski, immediately and inevitably called "Ski" by his hutmates, was a tall, husky New Yorker who had worked as a telephone lineman. Such men often were selected for machine gun duty because of their obvious physical strength and endurance, and Ski, too, was assigned to M Company.

Harris and his fellow gunners' training initially involved classroom instruction on the nomenclature, function, and care and cleaning of the Browning, but the Marines were soon putting their knowledge into practice at Camp Lejeune's machine gun ranges and on live-firing areas in the expansive "boondocks" of coastal North Carolina. Over the coming

Ayresie and Tom Savery, Camp Lejeune, late fall, 1942

weeks and months, each man would learn and master the duties of every member of the Browning heavy machine gun crew as it moved, emplaced the weapon, fired, and moved again.

The "gunner" or "number one gunner" carried the fifty-pound tripod, which formed a stable base for the weapon. This crew member became accustomed to carrying the tripod for miles, walking or running when necessary, with the tripod's front two legs held over his shoulders like a steel yoke. When directed by his squad or section leader, the number one gunner placed the tripod in the assigned position and general direction of fire.

The "assistant" or "number two" gunner carried the thirty-caliber weapon, itself almost a fifty-pound load, and lowered and secured its pinion into a socket in the emplaced tripod. By this time, the number one gunner had moved into position to orient and aim the weapon.

The number two gunner, after attaching the weapon to its tripod, placed a metal, rectangular box of belted 30.06 ammunition on the ground to the left of the now fully mounted and oriented weapon. This handler, or a water carrier if available, also placed a metal water container and hose at the tripod's base and connected the hose to the cooling jacket to capture steam formed as the twenty-four-inch barrel inside heated during firing. The number two gunner inserted the belted ammunition into the weapon's receiver, making certain that the ammunition fed properly into the weapon.

In a skilled crew, all of these movements were performed in a smooth and continuous sequence, lasting only a few seconds once the firing position and orientation were established by the squad or section leader. Experience had proven that combat would not always permit these well-rehearsed movements to be performed by a machine gun squad serving at full strength. Thus, each man learned and mastered every crew member's duties and even practiced performing duties single-handedly.

The ability to perform these tasks quickly at less than full strength was not taught and learned to meet a hypothetical need. Ayresie, Bob Avery, Tom Savery, and "Ski" Rutkowski learned that during a three-day period in late October of 1942, less than two weeks after they had been assigned to M Company, Marine Sergeants John Basilone and Mitchell Paige each had carried on alone when all other members of their machine gun sections had been killed or wounded. These Marines manned and fired their Browning water-cooled heavies single-handedly for hours, killing dozens of Japanese soldiers attempting to overrun their positions on the island of Guadalcanal. For their actions, both Marines were awarded the Congressional Medal of Honor.

Mastering the Browning heavy was a complex and difficult task which required frequent range and field firing. The machine gunners learned to provide accurate direct or "grazing" fire, in which the trajectory of the rounds never rose above the height of a visible human target. They also learned and practiced "indirect fire." For this technique, a distant observer adjusted higher angle or "plunging" fire so that it fell in a "beaten zone" on a target masked by terrain and entirely out of sight of the machine gun crew.

Of course, Marines assigned to crew-served weapons also carried individual weapons for close-in defense of their positions. Ayresie's crew already had trained and qualified with the 1903 Springfield rifle. However, these weapons were too large and cumbersome to carry and use as the men moved and served their machine gun and its supply of ammunition and accessories. As machine gunners the Marines of Company M were issued lighter, short-barreled M55 Reising guns, capable of selective automatic or semiautomatic fire. Their training quickly expanded to include familiarization and qualification with this weapon.

As the late fall of 1942 lengthened and winter approached, Company M's training expanded to include combined arms maneuvers, in which infantry battalions and machine gun units worked in close coordination with artillery, tanks, and even aircraft, which made low level, simulated strafing runs in support of ground attacks. In all such exercises, Company M's machine gunners kept pace with infantry units on long marches through Camp Lejeune's boondocks, their load of individual weapons and field equipment increased by the substantial bulk and weight of the Browning, its tripod, ammunition, and water supply. On long marches, the gunners often pulled T-handled two-wheeled carts containing their weapon, ammunition, water, and spare parts.

The machine gunners of M Company developed a certain panache as they willingly bore their extra burdens. Most even came to feel affection for their weapons. In October of 1942, Harris wrote to Harriette Weston, enclosing a picture of the Browning on its tripod. On the reverse side of this picture, Ayresie wrote, "This is the baby that will give the Japs hell!" Bob Avery mailed a copy of the same picture to his parents, signing his letter, "Machine Gun Bob," and assuring them that the "Japs will know we are a hard bunch when we hit them." Bob labeled the photographed gun, "my sweetie."

In preparation for their future amphibious assaults, the Twenty-Third Regiment practiced landing over Camp Lejeune's Atlantic coastline from various amphibious landing craft. Most of their early amphibious training involved "hitting the beach" from LCVPs (Landing Craft, Vehicle, Personnel), sometimes called "Higgins" boats. These diesel powered, shallow draft boats, thirty-six feet in length, had been designed by their namesake, Andrew Jackson Higgins of New Orleans. Each LCVP, unlike earlier versions of the craft, called "LCPs," was equipped with a steel bow ramp, which could drop quickly to allow troops to rush ashore as soon as the craft grounded on the beach of an objective.

*M1917 A2 machine gun outside the squad's
hut at Camp Lejeune, late 1942.*

The Marines very rarely stepped ashore onto dry sand. More often than not, they plunged into waist-deep water off the LVCP ramp and slogged ashore through chilly ocean water while keeping their weapons and ammunition dry. As soon as the troops had cleared the ramp, the Higgins boat's shallow draft, in theory if not always in practice, allowed its crew to raise the bow ramp, reverse off the beach, and return to deeper water.

In late November and December of 1942, the Twenty-Third Regiment began to train for all phases of the amphibious assault, including laborious disembarkation from amphibious assault ships called "APAs." From their quarters deep in the ship's holds, where close layers of bunks were often stacked four high, the ship's public address system summoned them by boat teams to one of several boat stations located along the port and starboard sides of the APA's main deck. Heavy cargo nets were rigged over the ship's sides from each boat station extending downward to LCVPs holding their positions below. The fully armed and equipped Marines swung over the rail and mounted the nets. Gripping only the vertical rope strands to avoid having their hands stepped on by other combat loaded men descending above them, the Marines carefully stepped downward, placing their boondockers on horizontal strands until they reached the decks of the LCVP below.

Even moderate swells caused the LCVPs to heave upward three feet and more, and then quickly drop. The boat's crew, and then the first Marines to descend the net, quickly hauled on the outboard ropes of the net, holding it as taut as they could to clear the pitching gunwales of the LCVP. Marines attempted to step quickly downward onto the deck of the LCVP at the precise top of its rise to minimize the impact, and avoid falling in a heap to the deck. Accidents, including falls from the cargo net into the treacherous, narrow space between the sides of the APA and the LCVP, occurred on some occasions. The unfortunate Marine usually was promptly rescued, suffering only a complete drenching and loss of his weapon.

As soon as the boat team of up to thirty-six Marines was fully loaded, the cargo net was cast away against the side of the APA, enabling the next LCVP to arrive below the boat station. The loaded LCVP pulled away as an empty LCVP arrived, and the process was repeated.

As the LCVPs departed from the APA with their load of troops, they joined a circling group of others and together formed a "wave" that would proceed in line for the assault on the hostile shore. Such circling might last for hours until a signal hoist from a control vessel directed the circling draft to proceed in a column toward their line of departure.

In response to yet another signal, the column of LCVPs formed into a line, and with engines roaring, crossed the line of departure and made their run to the beach at a top speed of nine to twelve knots.

As each LCVP approached the beach, the boat team leader, who was the senior officer or NCO aboard, ordered the troops to "lock and load" their weapons. At this command, all aboard, either actually or in simulation during training, chambered a round of ammunition and engaged the weapon's safety to prevent an accidental discharge. As the ramp dropped and the boat team quickly cleared the landing craft, all personnel were trained to move beyond the high water mark, clear the beach, reorganize as quickly as possible into their regularly assigned units, and attack inland.

This intricate process, which required precise teamwork by thousands of naval and Marine Corps officers and men, was practiced repeatedly from beginning to end and under a variety of conditions until it became second nature.

The heavy regimen of field and amphibious training was occasionally interrupted when Marines were given passes or "liberty," enabling them to leave the base for a weekend, or granted "leave" for longer absences. On weekends Bob, Tom, and Ski, whenever sufficient funds were on hand, enjoyed liberty in Jacksonville, Morehead City, Wilmington, or other nearby North Carolina towns or cities. Greenville, North Carolina, where some 800 young women attended a state teacher's college, was the preferred destination of Bob Avery, who cut an impressive figure in his winter service uniform. Harris, ever faithful to his sweetheart, volunteered for guard duty or limited himself to visits to Camp Lejeune's theater or chaste forays into nearby Jacksonville.

As Christmas of 1942 approached, Harris and his hutmates listened to "White Christmas" and other seasonal songs on a radio an M Company Marine had acquired. Their thoughts turned increasingly to home and the possibility of extended leave. Each week, rumors circulated and leave authorizations were announced, only to be cancelled. Finally, on December 23, 1942, Harris, Bob, Tom, and Ski were authorized to take a full week of Christmas leave. They charged from camp to Jacksonville, North Carolina in their winter service uniforms, sporting their marksmanship badges. There, they crowded aboard northbound buses or trains and began long trips to their homes in New York and Pennsylvania.

If Harris and Nina Ayres and the Potts family, or the New York families of Bob, Tom, and Ski expected to see exhausted and ill-used sons and brothers on their arrival home, they were pleasantly surprised. Harris, for example, already strengthened by his steady farm work, stood straighter, seemed even stronger and more confident, and was in the words of the young, awestruck Delbert Potts, "solid as a rock." Tom Savery, ever the athlete, and Ski, now more powerful than ever, drew similar praise from relatives and friends. Bob Avery, who had weighed just over 160 pounds when he enlisted, now weighed a muscular 180. All of the men were lean and weathered by their constant field training.

Ayresie's parents put aside their differences during his leave and welcomed him home, marveling at his fit and robust appearance and his obvious pride in having become a Marine.

Harriette Weston had graduated from Union Endicott High School the previous June and was now working full time at the IBM Company in Binghamton, New York. She eagerly awaited her sweetheart's arrival.

Ayresie's reunion with Harriette, following a forced absence of almost five months, was as romantic and electric as one would expect. The determined Marine had only five days before he was to commence the return trip south to Camp Lejeune, and he made the most of them. Ayresie had saved the money that he might have spent on liberty trips with his squad mates. For Christmas, he surprised Harriette with a small diamond engagement ring. Harriette quickly accepted Ayresie's proposal, and their engagement to be married at an unspecified future date was announced.

On December 29, 1942, Harriette, now officially Ayresie's fiancée, watched him board a southbound train in Binghamton, New York, and depart for the return trip to North Carolina. Like other M Company Marines fortunate enough to take Christmas leave, Ayresie, Bob, Tom, and Ski concluded that their leave experiences were treasured and memorable, but ended far too quickly.

The returning Marines had neither time nor opportunity to mope upon their return to Camp Lejeune. Their field and machine gun training immediately resumed and intensified. New Year's Eve of 1942 was spent in the field, where Company M held live firing exercises.

During his Christmas leave, Ayresie had worked out a personal code with his mother and Harriette, so that his innocuous use of a certain family friend's name would indicate a predesignated location or destination. He soon made good use of this covert manner of communication. In January, "scuttlebutt" circulated that the Twenty-Third Marines would soon ship out to Iceland. A later rumor held that the regiment would recapture the Aleutian Islands, portions of which the Japanese had occupied shortly after their Pearl Harbor attack. Winter underwear and heavy wool shirts to be worn inside the cotton utility or field jackets were issued. In the bustle of activity, all further leaves were cancelled. Supplies and equipment were staged for embarkation. Troops' individual equipment and weapons were carefully inspected. Meanwhile, the men had no idea where they were bound.

On January 11, 1943, the entire Twenty-Third Marine Regiment was quickly moved by train to the US Navy's base at Norfolk, Virginia. However, all scuttlebutt that had swept the ranks proved false. In Norfolk, Ayresie's Third Battalion boarded the USS *Leonard Wood*, an APA that had participated in Operation Torch, the American invasion of North Africa. The *Leonard Wood*, with Ayresie, Bob, Tom, and Ski aboard, joined a large convoy consisting of an aircraft carrier, battleship, heavy cruisers, LSTs, destroyers, and other attack transports. Once at sea, the troops were informed that they were to participate in three weeks of large scale amphibious training exercises in Chesapeake Bay, whose waters were judged more secure from the diminished but still present threat posed by German U-boats off the Atlantic Coast.

The Twenty-Third Marines made multiple landings on Solomon's Island, Maryland, assaulting the beaches with infantry supported by tanks, halftracks, and light artillery. Carrier aircraft roared just overhead providing simulated close air support as the Marines attacked their assigned objectives through smoke screens.

Ayresie and Bob Avery wrote home, describing the large convoy and the impressive operation. Bob stated that the operation was "great sport, quite an experience, and well worth the effort." Bob also passed along more sobering news. A total of twelve Marines in the regiment had lost their lives in various ways in the large scale landings and maneuvers. One Marine had drowned when an LCI or "Landing Craft Infantry" substantially larger than an LCVP had collided with a loaded LCVP during darkness, slicing it cleanly in two and instantly dumping Ayresie, Bob, the boat's two-man crew, and all other occupants of the craft into the frigid waters of Chesapeake Bay. Fortunately, the collision occurred near the *Leonard Wood*, and its crew quickly brought search lights to bear, while other LCVPs in the immediate area hurried to rescue all of the Marines, save the one who was never recovered. Ayresie's squad thus experienced for the first time the death of one of their comrades—an experience that would eventually be repeated many times over.

After the repetitive landings and assaults drew to a close, the troops were granted a brief shore liberty in Norfolk, Virginia, which they denounced as a "swabbie town" for the prevalence of sailors in the bars, theaters, and other liberty haunts.

Before returning to Camp Lejeune, Harris and Bob rescued a friendly stray pup from the Norfolk docks and smuggled him aboard the *Leonard Wood*. Members of the squad hid the pup aboard, fed him with leftovers from the ship's galley, and carried him with them on the train returning to Camp Lejeune. "Oscar" became a content and well-fed mascot for the Marines who shared their hut with Ayresie, Bob, Tom, and Ski.

Ayresie in full winter service uniform with "Oscar." Note rifle expert's medal and qualification with other weapons.

In February of 1943, Ayresie and his company were pleased to be issued new M1 carbines, replacing the widely disfavored Reising guns as individual weapons for machine gunners and others manning crew-served weapons. The light, semiautomatic carbines, whose magazines held fifteen rounds of specially manufactured .30 caliber ammunition, were much preferred to the Reising gun. In fact, one entire Marine unit fighting on Guadalcanal was reported to have "lost their Reisings in combat"—to a man.

In late winter and early spring of 1943, the Twenty-Third Marines' field and weapons training was augmented by increased indoctrination in the tactics and the sadistic behavior of the Japanese forces they were likely to encounter in combat. The men watched and listened attentively as films and first hand reports of the First Marine Division's experiences on Guadalcanal were presented. The Marines learned of the Japs' devious enticement of Marine Colonel Goettge's patrol of twenty-five volunteers, which was lured to a distant location on Guadalcanal by a prisoner's false report of a Japanese unit's desire to surrender and receive medical treatment. Immediately upon their arrival in a landing craft, the patrol was attacked and annihilated. Only three members of the patrol escaped. The last member to survive by swimming out to sea glanced toward the shore and saw the blades of Japanese soldiers' Samurai swords flashing in the sun above the bodies of his comrades as they were cut to pieces.

This information was received and processed by the Marines not with fear, but with grim determination and cold fury. Having heard these and similar reports, the men became even more eager to bring death to their enemy. Bob Avery's attitude was typical of those of Harris and others in M Company. Bob wrote to his family on March 13, 1943, that the Marines on Guadalcanal had "carried on with the true spirit of fighting Marines, and added another glorious chapter to the already filled chapters of Marine history." He closed his letter, "When we carry the battle to the enemy, they will have even more reason to fear the Marines."

Late June of 1943 brought a brief but pleasant interruption to Ayresie's training. He was granted a second leave, and rushed home to spend a full week with Harriette, the Potts family, and his parents. Harris and Nina Ayres had formally separated two months before he arrived in Montrose. His reunion with each of his parents was more awkward than usual, but his disappointment at the accelerating deterioration of his parents' relationship was softened by the joy of reuniting with his fiancée, and with his "second family," the Potts, who proudly photographed him in his summer khakis as he crouched between young Norval and Delbert.

A new rumor greeted Ayresie upon his return from Montrose. The Twenty-Third Marines had been ordered to make all preparations for departing Camp Lejeune on twenty-four hours' notice. The "word" this time was that the regiment would help "recapture the Philippines." The eager and confident machine gunners of Mike Company were certain that they were just the men to do it. With clothing and equipment packed and weapons cleaned until spotless, the Marines stood poised and ready to depart westward from the Carolinas.

Private First Class Harris Ayres flanked by Norval
and Delbert Potts beside Forest Lake

Unlike all other rumors, the latest to circulate among the Twenty-Third Marines was inaccurate only in some respects. Ayresie, Bob, Tom, and Ski certainly were leaving Camp Lejeune, and soon.

CHAPTER 4

WEST BY LAND

In early July of 1943, Ayresie, Bob, Tom, and Ski boarded one of thousands of troop trains operated by American railroad companies during World War II. In a remarkable display of altruism and patriotic cooperation, these fierce competitors shared their tracks and equipment as they carried hundreds of thousands of American troops to distant bases and ports of embarkation.

After comfortably settling aboard their Pullman cars, the Marines began a six-day trek westward to the sunny Southern California coast and a new 130,000 acre Marine Corps base at Camp Joseph Pendleton, some forty-five miles south of Los Angeles.

During Ayresie's 1942 train trip from New York to Parris Island, he first had seen the mid-Atlantic states and the southeastern low country. However, the sojourn by rail across the entire breadth of the North American continent from sea to shining sea truly amazed Ayresie and his three buddies. After the troop train emerged from the heat and humidity of the southeastern sunbelt, the men gaped for hours through large Pullman car windows at the passing spectacles of the rugged Texas panhandle, the Staked Plains or "Llano Estacado," where Comanches and Kiowas had raided and hunted a century and more before, and the impressive canyons, deserts, and mesas of New Mexico. Their troop train crossed the Continental Divide formed by the towering southern Rocky Mountains, descended to the colorful sands and buttes in and near Arizona's Painted Desert, and approached a Santa Fe Railroad spur line serving Camp Pendleton. The trip was a new and exciting experience that the young Marines would long remember.

During their scenic trip from Camp Lejeune, the Marines slept in bunks alongside their weapons. Because their troop train lacked a dining car, they ate excellent meals served by attractive "Harvey Girls" on fine china and linen at the many popular Harvey House restaurants located along their route.

On other trains, and on troopships sailing from the East Coast through the Panama Canal, the Twenty-Third Marines and other units converged on Camp Pendleton. The Twenty-Third would be joined by two other infantry regiments, the Twenty-Fourth and Twenty-Fifth Marines; by an artillery regiment, the Fourteenth Marines; by an engineering and pioneer regiment, the Twentieth Marines; and by other supporting units. All would combine to form a brand new Marine division—the Fourth. This division would train continuously for six months in Camp Pendleton's rolling hills and ravines, and on its flatlands and shores in preparation for amphibious assaults against the Japanese-held islands in the central Pacific.

Ayresie's regiment was housed in newly constructed two story barracks at Camp Pendleton. Other units were housed in large "tent cities" on the sprawling base. Their assigned quarters made little difference. All Fourth Division units spent most of their time in the field. In addition to participating in field and amphibious exercises, long marches and weapons training, the Marines were called on to fight frequent wildfires, which sprang up in Pendleton's arid training areas, often as not the result of live firing and explosives.

Camp Pendleton's seventeen miles of Pacific coastline and nearby San Clemente Island provided excellent opportunities for practice landings in LCVPs and tracked landing vehicles, called "LVTs," and in larger assault crafts, including the LCM or "Landing Craft Medium." On several landing exercises, the large guns of naval vessels fired overhead as assault waves moved toward their beach objective in realistic simulation of invasions to come.

In addition to their work on land and sea, the Marines of the Fourth Division trained and practiced *in* the sea. A variety of combat swimming exercises taught them to survive in ocean waters in the event of accidents or loss of their assault craft. Ayresie, who had frequented the waters of Forest Lake in Susquehanna County almost since birth, and Bob, his near equal in aquatic skills, had less trouble than many of their mates, including the hydrophobic Tom Savery. However, all learned to swim to shore through rough surf with their clothing and equipment and to swim a considerable distance underwater while holding their breath. The Marines also practiced jumping from a platform whose height above water matched that of a ship's deck. The need for these skills would become apparent to Ayresie, Bob, Tom, and Ski in the future.

Camp Pendleton's Marines were granted many opportunities to visit Los Angeles, San Diego, and other off-base destinations on weekend liberty. Ayresie chose not to take advantage of these opportunities, remained in camp to volunteer for guard duty, and preserved his pay and himself for his future marriage. Lacking such restraints, Bob, Tom, Ski, and practically every other single and unattached man, bolted eagerly off base at every opportunity, hitchhiking or riding buses to the alluring nightclubs and bars of Hollywood and Los Angeles to the north or San Diego to the south.

While Ayresie stoically remained on base, Bob, in particular, regularly enjoyed forays into the Los Angeles area. There, with other Marines, he relished the amenities of the Hollywood canteen, the Hollywood Grove where he met and befriended bandleader Freddie Martin, and Earl Carrolls. Bob described this particular nightclub to his mother as home of "the most beautiful girls in the world." Bob so favorably impressed one Los Angeles lass and her family that he was invited to stay at their home on subsequent visits. Bob and "Dottie" enjoyed horseback riding, hiking, and swimming together. Bob described these pleasant experiences in several letters home, constantly assuring his mother that the relationship was "nothing serious."

Private First Class Bob Avery and friend share their Los Angeles table with two of Bob's Mike Company buddies, Privates William Murrin and Michael Mallick of Clifton, New Jersey.

The Division's rigorous training schedule, the many and varied rumors of imminent departure, and the vast distance between the east and west coasts offered no hope to Ayresie or his comrades from New York that they might be able to spend Christmas of 1943 at home with their families and loved ones. Faced with those circumstances the Twenty-Third Marines, especially those too far from their eastern homes to visit on a brief wartime leave, became more and more impatient to get moving and do their part against the Japanese.

In late November and early December of 1943, sobering news through official and unofficial channels reached Camp

Pendleton. These reports described the American invasion of a Japanese-held Pacific island that would become both famous for its outcome and controversial for its cost.

On November 20, 1943, the Second Marine Division assaulted the northern beaches of Betio, a small island in Tarawa Atoll in the Gilbert Islands. This island, although barely more than a square mile in area and only a few hundred yards wide at its broadest point, was extremely well fortified and heavily defended by some 5,000 Japanese, including Japanese "Special Naval Landing Forces." These "Japanese marines" were reputed to be Japan's most aggressive and tenacious fighters.

An extensive preinvasion area bombardment by low trajectory naval guns had been ineffective against the enemy's reinforced concrete bunkers, and hundreds of buried gun emplacements strengthened by layers of thick coconut logs and sand. To make matters worse, the available American intelligence had substantially overestimated the depth of water over Betio's fringing northern reef, and an inadequate number of tracked LVTs had been provided.

The initial assault waves aboard LVTs quickly negotiated the shallow waters over Betio's coral reef and successfully delivered most of their troops to the invasion beaches. However, later waves of Marines aboard LCVPs, which grounded on the reef and could proceed no further, were forced to leap off their crafts into chest or neck-deep water and struggle hundreds of yards to shore, while deadly Japanese machine gun and anti-boat fire swept their ranks. These attacking Marines had suffered severe casualties. Somber news reports and films of dead Marines floating in the surf caused revulsion among the civilian population.

The bravery of the Marines at Tarawa, who steadfastly waded shoreward through deadly machine gun fire with their weapons held high and dry, certainly added to the proud history and tradition of the Marine Corps. Nevertheless, the reports raised legitimate concerns, and preparation and techniques would quickly evolve to address problems that arose at Tarawa.

Although certainly difficult and resulting in more casualties than anticipated, the Tarawa invasion was a clear American victory and a devastating defeat for the Japanese. Admiral Keiji Shibasaki, who commanded the Japanese troops on Betio, boasted that "a million men could not take Tarawa in a hundred years." The Second Marine Division secured the island in seventy-six hours, killing virtually all of the island's 5,000 man garrison. Only 446 defenders, seventeen of whom were Japanese, survived. 1,115 Marines were killed in action, while 2,292 were wounded.

Guadalcanal's jungle campaign had been difficult and protracted, but the First Marine Division's initial landing there was not opposed. The Second Division's bloody assault on Tarawa was the first Pacific amphibious landing that was opposed by the Japanese at the water's edge. Fewer casualties might well have been suffered with any combination of accurate advance intelligence about reef and beach conditions, more effectively targeted preinvasion bombardment, and a greater number of LVTs for use by the assault waves. In addition, more robust communication equipment capable of withstanding immersion and the concussive effects of friendly and enemy fire would have helped matters.

While no opposed amphibious assault would ever be free of risks or casualties, Ayresie, Bob, and the other Marines of the Fourth Division were confident that lessons learned at Betio would result in improved equipment and techniques for future invasions. Bob Avery wrote from Camp Pendleton that these changes would assure that "the tragedy of Tarawa will not be repeated."

With the reports from Tarawa received and processed, and all hope of Christmas leave gone, M Company's young machine gunners received inoculations against Pacific diseases and readied their weapons and ammunition. On Christmas Day, Ayresie, Bob, Tom, and Ski enjoyed a turkey dinner with "all the trimmings" in their mess hall.

On December 29, 1943, M Company, following a twenty-two mile conditioning hike, was ordered to pack their seabags and stand by with their weapons and equipment for departure. Scuttlebutt held that the Fourth Division would be shipped out to China. Within days, M Company boarded trucks, pulled away from their barracks, and turned south outside Camp Pendleton's gate. Ayresie and the Marines of M Company were now outbound, their destination unknown.

CHAPTER 5

WEST BY SEA

On January 12, 1944, Ayresie, hoisting his carbine, field equipment, and packed sea bag, mounted the gangplank of the USS *Calvert*, an APA docked in San Diego Bay. This vessel, commissioned only some fifteen months before, already had carried American soldiers across the Atlantic to the invasions of North Africa and Sicily, and had returned to transport troops to Makin Island at Tarawa Atoll in November of 1943.

Unlike their previous embarkations at Norfolk and San Diego, the Marines' purpose was not to conduct practice landings at San Clemente Island or on other American shores. The *Calvert* now was combat-loading the Third Battalion, Twenty-Third Marines, called "Battalion Landing Team 3/23" or "BLT 3/23." The scale of embarkations at San Diego left no doubt that the Fourth Marine Division's extensive training in North Carolina and California would be put to the test of combat.

The following day, January 13, 1944, the *Calvert* departed San Diego bound westward into the Pacific. Not until the convoy bearing the Fourth Division had been at sea for several days was their objective revealed.

USS Calvert, APA 32. The Calvert was typical of World War II attack transports that carried American troops thousands of miles to enemy shores in North Africa, Europe, and the Pacific. Note two LCVPs held by davits on her starboard side and the painted odd numbers below deck level. These enabled coxswains operating LCVPs to identify and approach their assigned boat stations.

The American Pacific strategy called for the United States Marines to advance across the Pacific to seize island objectives held by the Japanese forces. This island-hopping campaign would continue until American forces conquered and held positions close enough to launch and support a decisive attack against Japan's home islands. In this fashion the United States would, in the words of Commander-in-Chief Franklin D. Roosevelt, "win through to absolute victory."

Selection of Pacific island objectives was based on the need to neutralize Japanese interdiction of operations in other areas of the Pacific, on the target's strategic value in supporting further advances toward the Japanese home islands, and particularly on the objective's suitability as a base for American naval and air forces, including bombers and their fighter escorts.

Consistent with these principles, Guadalcanal, the Northern Solomon Islands, and Tarawa were attacked and conquered. Their seizure eliminated Japan's ability to interfere with America's supply lines to Australia, and provided air fields and deep draft harbors to support further attacks to the north and west against Japan.

Following the swift but bloody capture of Tarawa, the next logical step toward Japan, and the objective of Operation Flintlock was to seize a strategic link in Japan's outer ring of defenses in the Marshall Islands. The Japanese command center in the Marshalls was located in Kwajalein's 650 square mile atoll. A vital airfield from which Japanese bombers had attacked Wake Island in December of 1941 was located on the Island of Roi, one of two small, connected islands at the northern end of Kwajalein Atoll.

Ground troops in Operation Flintlock against the Marshall Islands would mount a two-pronged attack with separate task forces. The Northern Task Force would assault and capture Roi and its nearby twin, Namur. The Southern Task Force would seize the island of Kwajalein at the southern end of Kwajalein Atoll.

The Fourth Marine Division, including Ayresie's BLT 3/23, constituted the Northern Task Force assigned to attack Roi and Namur, destroy the Japanese defenders, and turn over the conquered islets to aviation units who would operate Roi's prized airfield.

Roi's entire land area of one square mile was devoted to the runways and taxiways of its sizeable airfield and to an administrative building, hangars, and other minor support structures. Namur, Roi's neighbor to its immediate east, was connected to Roi by a paved causeway and by a narrow, natural sandspit. The Japanese had erected numerous buildings and other structures on Namur, including the Japanese military headquarters for the Marshall Islands. With these structures, and more broken, irregular terrain with substantial undergrowth, Namur was better suited for defense against ground attack than its neighbor.

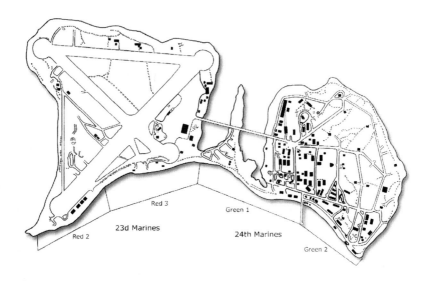

Red 3

Green 1

23d Marines

Red 2

24th Marines

Green 2

The Fourth Marine Division's assault of Roi and Namur was the first operation in which an American unit had departed from the United States and traveled directly to assault an enemy objective. The division traveled some 4,900 miles aboard its convoy from San Diego to Kwajalein Atoll. The convoy anchored only briefly at Lahaina Roads, a protected anchorage off Maui in the Hawaiian Islands, to refuel and reprovision. No troops were allowed ashore.

During the eighteen day voyage westward Ayresie, Bob, and Ski settled into a monotonous shipboard routine. Their Browning heavy machine gun and their individual weapons were repeatedly cleaned, oiled, and inspected. Bayonets and "KA-BAR" combat knives were sharpened to a razor edge. The troops engaged in daily calisthenics on deck to ward off the effects of physical inactivity forced by their close confinement.

The routine of the unfortunate Tom Savery was less active than that of his buddies. The moment the outbound *Calvert* encountered the ocean swells outside San Diego Bay, Tom, like some other Marines, fell victim to seasickness. For Tom this misery continued until the *Calvert* approached and entered the sheltered lagoon of Kwajalein Atoll.

Over 1,000 men of BLT 3/23 were embarked aboard the *Calvert*. The Marines stood in line for hours, waiting their turn for meals served below on the crowded mess deck, for occasional opportunities to purchase candy or "pogey bait" and other items from the small ship's store, and to use the troop head during the limited hours when fresh water might be available.

As soon as Operation Flintlock's convoy passed beyond the Hawaiian Islands, troop briefings commenced. Roi and Namur shared similarities with Tarawa. All three islands were small, and protected by numerous large caliber guns and automatic weapons emplaced in sturdy fortifications and trenches. Roi and Namur were defended by a substantial, well-armed, and determined Japanese force.

Planners of Operation Flintlock logically assumed that Roi and Namur would be defended as fiercely as the Japanese had defended Tarawa. Senior commanders were determined that Tarawa's mistakes contributing to the heavy Marine casualties would be minimized. Changes and adjustments were made. Preinvasion supporting fires would be enhanced. The shortage of LVTs at Tarawa would be remedied.

As Operation Flintlock's convoy approached Kwajalein Atoll, US Army Air Corps and naval aircraft attacked Japanese ships and airbases in the area, as well as Roi and Namur themselves. This bombardment from the air continued for several days, until January 31, 1944, D Day for Operation Flintlock.

While planning the Tarawa invasion, General Julian Smith, commanding the Second Marine Division, had strongly suggested that the neighboring island of Bairiki, 500 yards to the east of Betio, be taken as an initial objective and used as a land base for artillery bombardment of Betio by the howitzers of the Tenth Marines. The Amphibious Corps commander at Tarawa, General Holland M. Smith, had rejected this proposal, reasoning that delaying the attack on Betio in order to capture Bairiki would risk an attack on troop-bearing transports by Japanese air and naval forces. General Smith also concluded that the Second Marine Division could ill afford to commit one of its three infantry regiments to the capture of Bairiki.

These concerns had been overcome for the Fourth Division's invasion of Roi and Namur. In the first phase of the northern attack force's operation, the Twenty-Fifth Marines would seize and occupy five small islands flanking Roi and Namur to the southeast and southwest. The Fourteenth Marines would then land to supplement air and naval bombardment of Roi and Namur with land-based artillery fire.

In the predawn darkness of January 31, 1944, the *Calvert* and other ships bearing the troops of the Fourth Division hove to just outside the lagoon of Kwajalein Atoll to the west of Roi and Namur. For several hours, Ayresie, Bob, and Ski, now joined by Tom, whose seasickness had finally abated in the calmer waters, heard and observed for the first time from the *Calvert's* main deck the explosions, fire, and smoke of a concentrated and sustained preinvasion bombardment of an enemy shore by naval gunships and aircraft.

While the *Calvert* remained on station throughout January 31, 1944, elements of the Twenty-Fifth Marines seized the small islands that flanked Roi and Namur. Artillerymen of the Fourteenth Marines then landed and placed their howitzers in position to support the invasion of Roi and Namur, scheduled for the first of February.

Ayresie and his companions aboard the *Calvert* were awakened before dawn on February 1, 1944, and fed the Marines' traditional preinvasion breakfast of steak and eggs. The machine gunners of Company M already had learned that the First and Second Battalions of the Twenty-Third Marines would assault from the lagoon the eastern and western halves, respectively, of Roi's southern shore, while BLT 3/23 would be held in reserve. Just to the east, BLTs 2/24 and 3/24 would assault Namur.

As dawn finally broke on February 1, 1944, Ayresie and Bob watched silently as assault waves of Marines, visible in the distance, moved aboard LCVPs to LSTs that had entered Kwajalein's lagoon. There, they transferred to LVTs which would carry them ashore in the assault. Ayresie's squad could only wait and watch, fully armed and equipped, and wonder if they would be called on to land on Roi in support of the leading assault troops.

The assault companies of BLTs 1/23 and 2/23 waited at their line of departure for almost an hour until the waves of the Twenty-Fourth Marines had formed to their east for their attack on Namur. Finally, the waves of Marines aboard their LVTs raced toward both shores, while rocket-firing LCIs and armored LVTs called LVT(A)s firing thirty-seven millimeter guns, led the way. Supporting artillery fire from the flanking islands, naval gun fire from offshore, and aerial bombardment continued to pound the twin islands until the last possible moment.

On Roi, the leading wave of LVT(A)s crossed Red Beach at 1133 hours and immediately turned their guns on reinforced Japanese concrete blockhouses near the shore.

Minutes later, BLTs 1/23 and 2/23 hit Roi's southern beach. To their complete surprise there was little or no Japanese resistance. It was soon apparent that the prolonged aerial and naval gunfire bombardment, supplemented by the Fourteenth Marines' artillery fire from neighboring islands, had devastated Roi. Many of its Japanese defenders had fled eastward across the narrow causeway to Namur to seek better shelter from the intense naval and air bombardment.

Only a few hundred determined Japanese troops remained on Roi to fight the invading Marines, now facing enemy troops after almost a year of hard training and indoctrination. In the absence of appreciable resistance on or near the beach, the assault elements advanced quickly inland some 300 yards to the first day's designated objective on Roi, a preestablished map boundary called the "O-1 line." Here, the troops had been instructed to halt, guard against a potential counterattack, and await further orders to advance.

Within a few minutes after the initial landings, the Twenty-Third Marines' commanding officer, Colonel Louis Jones, radioed Fourth Division Commanding General Harry Schmidt aboard his command ship and reported, "This is a pip…no opposition near the beach." Soon afterward, Colonel Jones radioed again, "O-1 ours. Give us the word and we will take the rest of the island."

Such word was not forthcoming from General Schmidt's headquarters afloat. However, the absence of orders to advance against the enemy gave not a moment's pause to the charged up and aggressive Marines. Several LVT(A)s, joined by M3 light tanks that had landed, began to advance northward, firing on Japanese defenders. The riflemen of BLTs 1/23 and 2/23, supporting the advancing tanks and LVT(A)s as they were trained to do, surged over the invisible 0-1 line, either destroying or isolating small pockets of Japanese resistance.

At 1230 hours, BLT 3/23 aboard the *Calvert*, including Company M, whose separate machine gun platoons had been attached to the landing team's three infantry companies, were ordered to board LCVPs and land immediately in support of the First and Second Battalions ashore. Ayresie as an acting squad leader, Tom as his number one gunner, Ski as number two gunner, and Bob as ammunition bearer, reported to their assigned boat station, climbed down cargo nets into their LCVPs, and by 1300 had landed on Roi.

The scene that greeted them was not as expected. Unlike Tarawa, no torn bodies of dead Marines were present. Substantial supplies were already being delivered and stacked ashore. Occasional shots rang out as Ayresie's machine gun squad was ordered to the eastern shore of Roi. There, they placed their Browning heavy machine gun to defend against any Japanese counterattack or infiltration from Namur, to engage targets of opportunity on Roi's northeastern corner, and if called upon, to support the northward advance on Namur.

Soon after Ayresie and his crew had crossed Roi's beach and placed their Browning heavy, the spontaneous attack of the First and Second Battalions in support of the advancing LVT(A)s and tanks had closely approached Roi's northern shore, killing many Japanese troops in the process. General Schmidt concluded that these Marines had succeeded too well on Roi by taking the initiative in a determined but disorganized and potentially costly demonstration of aggressive fighting spirit. Frantic observers already were ordering supporting artillery and naval guns to cease fire, lest they strike the eagerly attacking troops on Roi.

General Schmidt, determined to restore order and implement the division's carefully crafted operation plan for securing

Roi and Namur in phases, ordered Colonel Jones to get his tanks, LVTs, and troops back behind the O-1 line and await further orders. This withdrawal and reorganization took some time, but all armored and infantry units that had attacked across the O-1 line were back in place by 1530. BLTs 1/23 and 2/23 then attacked northward along the east and west coasts of Roi, while BLT 3/23's rifle companies and machine gunners mopped up, dislodging and destroying isolated and concealed defenders who had been bypassed in the rapid attack northward.

Although little remained of the battle for Roi as Ayresie and his crew took position, their mission was not without danger. The entire Third Battalion was under sporadic Japanese fire during February 1 and 2. Ayresie's crew fired bursts from their Browning at Japanese troops moving to the north on Namur, and on some Japanese observed near the sandspit connecting Roi and Namur. A burst fired by gunner Tom Savery either drove the few observed Japanese soldiers back under cover, or killed or "silenced" them. As Bob Avery moved forward with ammunition, a Japanese Arisaka rifle round pierced his canvas gas mask carrier, narrowly missing him.

Just after 1800 on February 1, 1944, Roi Island was declared secured. The Twenty-Third Marines had crushed the Japanese resistance on the island in some six hours—a remarkable feat, particularly in view of the delayed landing and further delays in recalling the invaders from their initial advance, reorganizing them, and recommencing the attack northward.

On Namur, the Twenty-Fourth Marines were having a more difficult time. Namur lacked Roi's extensive flat runways and taxiways. It held numerous protected positions from which concealed Japanese gunners engaged attacking Marines, even though most of their heavy gun positions had been destroyed by the preinvasive bombardment. The LVT(A)s supporting the assault waves of the Twenty-Fourth Marines encountered anti-tank ditches and other barriers. Prevented from advancing ahead of the attacking infantry, the LVT(A)s could only fire in support of the assault troops until they advanced and became exposed to their supporting fire.

Nevertheless, the Twenty-Fourth Marines attacked vigorously against stronger Japanese resistance on Namur to their own O-1 line, an eastward extension of the same 0-1 map line across which the Twenty-Third Marines first had stormed on Roi.

Shortly after 1300 hours, Marines of BLT 2/24 attacking to the north on Namur encountered a substantial reinforced concrete building near the 0-1 line. The Marines placed charges against the building's outer wall, and spotted Japanese troops fleeing northward from the area. The initial explosive charge opened a breach in the building's concrete wall, and more powerful satchel charges were thrown inside the opening.

Suddenly the building vaporized and vanished in a massive explosion, followed by two secondary explosions. The satchel charges had triggered the explosion of stored Japanese torpedo warheads, bombs, and possibly other explosives within the building. The attacking Marines clearly had been unaware of this fact. The closest two dozen Marines were killed instantly. Another hundred, including the commander of BLT 2/24, were seriously wounded by the massive blast, which sent chunks of palm trees and huge pieces of concrete hurtling hundreds of feet into the air and raining down on Namur and boats near its shores resulting in further casualties. This explosion, for which the enemy scarcely could claim credit, caused one half of the casualties suffered by BLT 2/24 on Namur.

Marines on Roi's southern beach observe the
aftermath of the explosion on Namur.

The Second Battalion required some time to reorganize after the tragic explosion in its sector, but the embattled unit, reinforced by BLT 3/23's Marines and tanks sent from Roi, soon continued the attack northward against the island's Japanese defenders.

At 1930 all troops on Namur were ordered to halt and tie in their defensive positions for the night. During the early morning hours of February 2, 1944 the Twenty-Fourth Marines repulsed a Japanese counter-attack, and then resumed their attack northward with tanks in support. In the course of this attack the commanding officer of CT 1-24, Lieutenant Colonel Aquilla Dyess, was killed leading his troops as they approached Namur's north shore.

Namur was declared secured at approximately 1400 on February 2, 1943. Shortly thereafter the Marines discovered dozens of dead Japanese troops in a trench near the northern shore. All had committed suicide, either by firing their rifles with their toes or by clasping exploding grenades to their chests, rather than surrender to the Americans. This behavior, considered strange by Marines trained and willing to fight until they were killed, reinforced their training and indoctrination on the lengths to which fanaticism would drive their enemy.

As the engineers of the Twentieth Marines began to repair and ready Roi's airfield for use, other Marines on both islands were ordered to bury the Japanese dead in mass graves. In addition to 597 wounded, 190 Marines were killed on Roi and Namur and buried in a Fourth Division cemetery quickly laid out on Roi Island. Over 3,400 Japanese lost their lives on Roi and Namur.

Ayresie, Bob, Tom, and Ski had survived unscathed, had engaged the enemy, and had experienced their first taste of combat. The only "casualty" among the four Marines was Bob Avery's gas mask carrier.

Although Ayresie's team had been involved in only a few hours of armed conflict, the entire experience had instilled in them a large measure of confidence and pride. Eventually, Congressional Medals of Honor were awarded to Lieutenant Colonel Aquilla Dyess and First Lieutenant John Power, who had led his platoon in a fierce attack against positions on Namur. Privates Richard Anderson on Namur and Richard Sorenson on Roi had thrown themselves on live grenades in order to protect their comrades and were also awarded Medals of Honor. Of these four Marines, only Private Sorenson survived to receive his award.

Many other Marines had made sacrifices, and the attacking forces had performed bravely and effectively. Bob Avery, after lightly describing his near miss on Roi, added, "A more loyal and braver bunch of men have never lived than these boys of my outfit. I am proud to be a member of them."

On November 3, 1944, M Company reboarded the *Calvert* and began a voyage eastward toward the Hawaiian Islands and the base that would serve as their home for the duration of the Pacific war.

CHAPTER 6

CAMP MAUI

Located between Oahu and the "Big Island" of Hawaii, Maui long has been regarded as one of the most exotic and beautiful islands on Earth. Its 727 square miles are formed by the unsubmerged peaks of two adjacent dormant volcanoes, joined by more level terrain. Peaks on the western portion rise to 6,700 feet above the Pacific Ocean. Mount Haleakala, which comprises much of Maui's eastern section, rises to over 10,000 feet. The two-mile gain in altitude from Maui's tropical seashore to the seasonally snow-capped peak of Mount Haleakala occurs within a few overland miles, resulting in a wide range of climate and flora within a dramatically short distance.

Before departing Roi in the Marshall Islands, Ayresie's team had been informed that they were bound for "Camp Maui." They briefly had admired Maui's beaches, tropical greenery, and exotic volcanic topography from the *Calvert's* deck as the invasion fleet, sailing westward in Operation Flintlock, lingered briefly to refuel and resupply at Lahaina Roads. The prospect of returning from Roi to Maui heightened their spirits.

On February 15, 1944, the Marines of BLT 3/23 drifted in groups to the *Calvert's* rail as the peaks of the Hawaiian Islands appeared on the eastern horizon. Before approaching Maui, the *Calvert*, in company with the transports *LaSalle* and *Doyne* bearing other landing teams of the Fourth Division, steered northward off Oahu and entered Pearl Harbor. More curious Marines gathered at the rail as it approached the dock area. To their surprise, an enthusiastic and cheering crowd had gathered. As their ship drew closer and lines were cast to secure it dockside, the crowd continued to wave and cheer while a uniformed US Navy band struck up "The Marines' Hymn." The Marines aboard responded with defiantly raised fists, cheers of their own, and many a dampened eye.

As soon as the *Calvert* was made fast, and as the band continued to serenade the Marines, a gangplank was raised and casualties were carefully evacuated. Among the evacuees was Bob Avery, who had experienced severe pain in his left side during the return voyage from Roi to Pearl Harbor. Bob was taken to the Aeia Heights Naval Hospital where doctors examined him, and told him he was suffering from kidney stones. One physician recommended that Bob be taken stateside for surgery. Bob refused, firmly stating to the medical officer that he would prefer more conservative treatment enabling him to remain with Ayresie and his other buddies in M Company, who, as Bob wrote, had become "like family" to him. The exasperated physician responded that he "never saw a bunch of men so eager to rejoin their outfit as you guys from the Fourth Division." Bob simply shrugged. After three weeks of treatment, his pain had subsided, and he impatiently awaited transportation from Pearl Harbor to Camp Maui.

After lingering overnight at Pearl Harbor, the *Calvert* made its way to Kahului Harbor on Maui's northern coast, where it arrived on February 17, 1944. The Marines hurriedly disembarked, organized into their companies and platoons, and boarded trucks in a constant flow carrying them from dockside through the fairgrounds and athletic fields near Kahului Harbor, and eastward along a palm and flame tree-fringed Macadam Road to Mount Haleakala's gentle northern slope. Here, 1,500 feet above the Pacific Ocean, lay Camp Maui, a rolling, open area which for the next twenty months would be the Fourth Marine Division's permanent home and training base between combat missions.

As luck would have it, Ayresie's Third Battalion had arrived on Maui in the midst of the rainy season. Thick, moist clouds, colliding with Maui's high mountain ranges, dumped torrents of rain on the island. Camp Maui's ordered rows of hundreds of M1934 walled pyramid tents now sat upon a sea of mud. The rains continued for days, as Ayresie and his squad slogged into their assigned tents and dumped their weapons and sea bags onto folding canvas cots.

As the entire Fourth Marine Division, over 17,000 strong, occupied Camp Maui, the Marines and their commanders turned to and began to make Camp Maui more livable. Wooden ammo and shipping crates were fashioned into decks for pyramid tents, makeshift chairs, and tables. Crushed stone was placed on pathways between tents and used to line gullies formed by the heavy rains.

Commanders saw to the erection of post exchanges, and shelters where troops could eat their chow out of the weather. Outdoor showers and wash stands were built. A public address system, crude by today's standards, was more than adequate to provide music for the enjoyment of the troops. Within two weeks, regimental outdoor theaters featured nightly motion pictures flown from stateside, and travelling USO shows. Marines sat on sandbag seats in orderly rows, and few retreated when the frequent showers came.

Within days the Fourth Marine Division resumed the same active training schedule that had been interrupted by the long voyage from San Diego to Kwajaleln Atoll and the return from Roi-Namur to Maui. Practice landings were regularly conducted at Maalaea Bay. The island contained no less than forty-seven separate training areas. Constant weapons training was conducted on Maui's various ranges with rifles, carbines, pistols, and submachine guns. Ranges also were available for grenades, flame throwers, mortars, and bazookas. Ranges for light and heavy machine guns, including Ayresie's Browning heavy, were soon up and running. An elaborate, rail-mounted moving target range was designed and built for thirty-seven millimeter antitank gunners.

Spacious areas along the coast permitted live firing and movement by tanks and LVT(A)s working in conjunction with Marine infantry units. Some areas contained pillboxes and concealed "enemy" emplacements modeled after Tarawa's defenses. Artillery positions and impact areas were available for the Fourteenth Marines. Mount Haleakala provided a grueling challenge for conditioning hikes scheduled for all hands.

Marine units underwent a fundamental reorganization following Operation Flintlock. As a result, on March 2, 1944, the Third Battalion's M Company, in which Ayresie and his squad had served for over a year, simply disappeared as an organization. At Roi, Company M's machine gun sections had been separated and attached to BLT 3/23's three infantry companies, I, K, and L. This made perfect sense. In combat, machine gun sections and squads worked with infantry units, not only providing strong and vital fire support in defensive positions, but also in support of assaults against the enemy. In either case, the mission of machine guns crews required close coordination and cooperation with infantry squads and platoons.

On March 2, 1944, a Twenty-Third Marine regimental order, similar to orders issued by all other Marine Regiments, disbanded all "M" or machine gun companies of the Twenty-Third Marines. M/3/23's machine gun sections became integral components of the Third Battalion's Companies I, K, and L. Ayresie, Bob, Ski, and Tom thus became members of I Company, Third Battalion, Twenty-Third Marines, or "I-3-23.". The machine gunners had routinely trained in joint exercises with the riflemen they supported, and had moved, emplaced, and moved again with them in Operation Flintlock. From now on they also would train, stand inspections, eat, sleep, and share their limited off duty hours with them.

In mid-March Ayresie received a pleasant surprise as Bob Avery rejoined his machine gun squad in I Company. During Bob's absence, Ayresie's natural leadership qualities had been observed both in training and in action. He was now a corporal and machine gun squad leader assigned to Company I.

This promotion had no apparent effect on Ayresie's friendship with Bob or others in his squad. These men had long respected Ayresie for his energy and competence, and for setting an aggressive pace in training, and in combat. Ayresie was blessed with the natural ability to lead and inspire without overbearing hostility or rancor.

Ayresie was no martinet. He was instead a "doer" who led by example and from the front. His affection for his buddies was unaffected by his responsibility as their squad leader. Ayresie and Bob remained particularly close and routinely reminisced while relaxing in their tent as Maui's rains fell, or while eating their rations in the field. While shooting pool together on liberty in Maui, they spoke often of their families, about Ayresie's fiancée, and their shared love of hunting and fishing along the border between New York and Pennsylvania. They enjoyed planning future outings in which they would try their luck together in the forests, streams, and fields at home after the war.

From mid-April to the second week of May, 1944, amphibious training began to play a more dominant role in the Fourth Division's schedule. Multiple full-phase landing exercises were conducted in which the Marines and their supporting arms boarded transports at Kahului Harbor, sailed around the island to Maalaea Bay, loaded onto landing craft, and assaulted beach and inland training objectives. These training activities were not random, but rather were designed in accordance with carefully crafted operation plans in preparation for the Fourth Division's next invasion, "Operation Forager," whose precise objective was then known only by senior commanders.

On May 13, 1944, Ayresie, Bob, Tom, and Ski left Camp Maui with other units in a truck convoy to Kahului Harbor. This time, in addition to the weapons and field equipment they carried on local amphibious exercises, they brought their packed sea bags for a long voyage. When Company I arrived at the docks of Kahului Harbor, they boarded LST 69, a "Landing Ship, Tank," instead of an APA attack transport. The reason was simple: BLT 3/23 would be one of the assault battalions for Operation Forager. In this operation, Ayresie's squad would sail to the objective aboard its LST, and on D-Day climb aboard an LVT and assault the objective.

Although LST 69's beam and length were 50 and 328 feet, respectively, troop accommodations for the officers and enlisted men aboard her were cramped and stifling. Many of the embarked Marines chose to relax and sleep under ponchos or shelter halves rigged from the many trucks, trailers, and other material loaded on the ship's exposed main deck.

LSTs, whose maximum speed under way was twelve knots, were in the slower portion of the massive convoy that eventually formed for Operation Forager. Because they required longer to reach assembly areas and the final objective, they embarked their troops and left port earlier than faster troop transports and fire support ships in the task force.

On May 20, 1944, LST 69 arrived at Pearl Harbor and entered the calm, tree-lined waters of West Loch, the large, western branch of the complex harbor system. There LST 69 moored side-by-side with several other LSTs. Eventually, twenty-nine LSTs bound for Operation Forager were closely grouped in six separate rows. This allowed more rapid loading and transfer of cargo and equipment onto, and sometimes off of the vessels. It also created a serious hazard.

All of the LSTs gathered in the West Loch were loaded with tons of their own fuel and ammunition. All manner of spare fuel and ammunition that would be needed by the embarked Marines also was closely stored on the ships' main decks. This massive concentration of volatile fuel and ammunition was deemed an acceptable risk in the preparations for Operation Forager.

After a quiet Saturday night aboard LST 69, Ayresie, Bob, Tom, and Ski spent Sunday morning, May 21, relaxing and tending to their weapons and equipment. By Sunday afternoon, they were lounging quietly on deck. Nearby, an army detachment stationed on Oahu was unloading mortar ammunition from LST 353.

For reasons not conclusively established to this day, a powerful explosion suddenly erupted in the immediate vicinity of the army work detail unloading the mortar shells from aboard LST 353. This unexplained mishap produced an enormous explosion, killed the laboring troops in the work detail, and showered flaming shards of steel and wreckage onto other closely-grouped LSTs in the West Loch. In a violent chain reaction, ship after ship exploded and burned, flinging still more fiery debris and further spreading the searing flames. One of the most closely guarded secrets of WWII, the "West Loch disaster," was well under way, and Ayresie and his squad were caught squarely in the middle of it.

The spreading flames and burning debris soon reached LST 69, where stored gasoline drums and fueled vehicles began to explode and burn. Its crew, like the crews of other LSTs in West Loch, fought the inferno as best they could. Some crews aboard outboard LSTs were able to cast their ships free and either start their engines or drift away from the concentrated flames and explosions. Others simply could not keep pace with the spreading explosions and flames. Throughout West Loch, crews and embarked troops were abandoning their vessels, and LST 69 was among the ships most involved in the disaster. The time clearly was nigh for Ayresie and his squad to escape their doomed vessel by leaping into the waters of West Loch and making their way to shore.

Ayresie gave the order and joined Bob and Ski, jumping as they had been trained from the burning deck into the water below. The three Marines surfaced among scattered patches of flaming oil and debris. Glancing upward to the deck they were horrified to see Tom Savery, ever the reluctant swimmer, still hesitating at the rail. As they treaded water, Ski screamed at the top of his lungs, "Savery, jump for God's sake!" Ayresie and Bob immediately added their strong voices to the urgent chorus.

Tom looked longingly at the shore of West Loch, glanced again at the rapidly approaching flames, and climbed slowly over the LST's rail. Pausing one last time, he jumped in the prescribed manner, clasping his nose with one hand and his crotch with the other. Tom plunged feet first into the water and surfaced sputtering. Ayresie and the others encouraged and assisted him as all four swam toward shore, occasionally ducking under the surface to avoid flaming oil and fuel.

The shore of West Loch was not far from LST 69, and Ayresie's squad, like hundreds of other sailors and Marines, soon reached land alive and uninjured. However, they now possessed only whatever sodden clothes they wore. Their spare clothing, personal effects, weapons, packs, and all equipment were lost in the burned and sunken wreckage of LST 69.

Many ships' crew members and others manned Higgins boats and other small craft and cruised about rescuing men who had leapt overboard. Many were saved, but some were not. Several rescued survivors and boat crews occasionally heard sickening thumps as the hulls of their vessels struck the bodies of victims in the water.

This disastrous conflagration and its accompanying explosions did not fully subside for over twenty-four hours.

Six LSTs, including LSTs 69 and 353, sank and were lost. Casualty reports vary widely. Between 163 and 392 men were reported to have died, including a number of Marines; 396 were reported to have been wounded.

Ill-fated LST 69 combat loaded and underway somewhere in the Pacific.

Operation Forager was subject to a carefully crafted schedule. Any significant delay would threaten to disrupt the American advance in the Pacific. The "second Pearl Harbor disaster" was quickly veiled in secrecy and classified Top Secret until the early sixties. Troops who had been aboard the lost LSTs, including Ayresie's squad, were hurriedly resupplied with their individual and crew-served weapons, dungarees, and all field equipment. Marines who had escaped LST 69 were quickly assigned to LST 19. Some troops aboard unaffected LSTs were given liberty in Honolulu. Other units conducted close order drill on the wharf near the scene of the disaster—a brave gesture intended to confirm "business as usual" to other troops and to Hawaiian civilians.

Remarkably, the Marines' departure aboard their LSTs from Hawaii was delayed only twenty-four hours by the West Loch disaster. On the afternoon of May 25, 1944 all LSTs in the slower portion of the convoy for Operation Forager departed Pearl Harbor, fully loaded with troops and their vehicles, weapons, ammunition, and equipment. The convoy was bound westward for the Marianas and another island whose name would take its own well-deserved place among others in Marine Corps history and tradition—Saipan.

CHAPTER 7

OPERATION FORAGER: THE ASSAULT ON SAIPAN

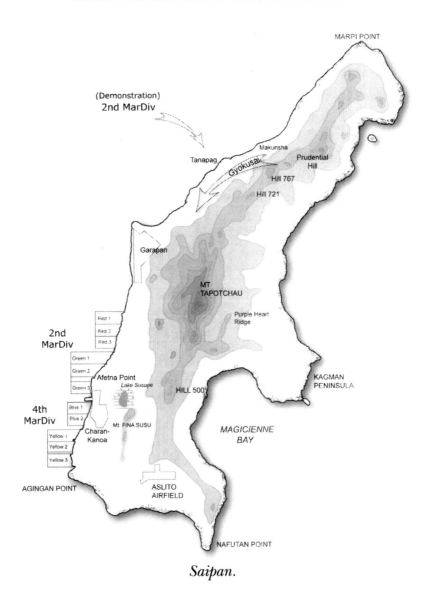

Saipan.

As May 25, 1944, drew to a close, Ayresie, Bob, Tom, and Ski settled again into a customary shipboard routine. LST 19, its main and well decks loaded with vehicles, fuel, LVTs, ammunition, and the newly rearmed and equipped Marines of I Company, plodded westward from Oahu at nine knots. Worn decks of cards were broken out for the ubiquitous games. Dog-eared paperback novels and magazines made the rounds and bull sessions resumed. From time to time, Marines admired the indescribably blue Pacific while dolphins raced and leapt in LST 19's bow wave.

LST 19 would require twenty-two days to reach the Marianas Island group. However, all was not languor and lassitude for the embarked Marines. Groups engaged in exercise sessions in shifts so that all aboard could vigorously perform calisthenics in the limited deck space. Troops stood the usual weapons and personnel inspections. Company and platoon commanders carefully briefed their men time and again about the coming operation and their units' assigned role in the attack.

Operation Forager against the Marianas, like Operation Flintlock in the Marshall Islands, would consist of a two-pronged attack. A Southern Landing Force consisting of the Third Marine Division and First Provisional Marine Brigade would seize the island of Guam. The Northern Landing Force comprised of the Second and Fourth Marine Divisions, with the US Army's Twenty-Seventh Infantry Division in reserve, would attack and seize Saipan and subsequently Tinian, its island neighbor to the immediate south.

Forager would bear little resemblance to the Fourth Division's quick and overwhelming capture of tiny Roi and Namur. As before, massive preinvasion naval and air bombardments would pound the beaches and other targets ashore until the last possible moment. Nevertheless, despite substantial Japanese troop and material losses to effective American submarine attacks, some 30,000 Japanese army and naval troops determined to resist the capture of this critical link in the "inner ring" of Japan's defenses were poised and ready on Saipan. Led by Japanese General Saito, they awaited the American's arrival with well-placed and concealed artillery and mortars, dozens of tanks, and countless automatic weapons.

Saipan's irregular coast framed seventy-two square miles, consisting of relatively level plains in the southern portion of the island, and jungled gorges, ridges, hills, and mountains in the central and northern portions. These features were far better suited for a strong defense than the flat terrain of Roi and Namur. Sugar cane fields in cultivated areas provided opportunities for frequent ambushes. The western coastal plains allowed the Japanese to employ their tanks. From positions in the central and northern caves, gorges, and hills, including 1,550 foot Mount Tapotchau, the Japanese could direct accurate artillery, mortar, and automatic weapons fire upon the attacking Americans. In Saipan's coastal capital city, Garapan, the Marines would fight in close quarters from building to building. Finally, the sheer size of Saipan presented a far greater challenge than Roi and Namur.

Two Marine divisions, Ayresie's Fourth, and the Second Marine Division, veterans of Guadalcanal and Tarawa, would assault Saipan's southwestern shore on D-Day, June 15, 1944, nine days following D-Day of Operation Overlord in Normandy, half a world away. Certain Second Division units who were not assigned to the main assault, and the Twenty-Fourth Marines, would participate in a feigned landing to the north at Tanapag Harbor. Naval gunfire would pound the beaches at the northern site. Landing craft would be lowered from troop transports and circle three miles from shore, but no assault troops would be aboard them. The desired effect of this demonstration was to convince Japanese units located near Tanapeg Harbor to remain in position. This limited goal was achieved. A full Japanese infantry regiment remained in the area until the mock invasion fleet withdrew.

The actual landings would occur simultaneously miles to the south, centered roughly on the northern outskirts of the coastal town of Charan Kanoa. On the left or northern portion of the invasion site, the Sixth and Eighth Marine regiments of the Second Marine Division would land on the Red and Green beaches. To their immediate right or south, Ayresie's Twenty-Third Marines, and the Twenty-Fifth Marines of the Fourth Marine Divisions, would land on the Blue and Yellow beaches.

BLT 3/23 would lead the assault on Blue Beach One. The first day's operation plan called for the Twenty-Third Marines' assault battalions to attack and secure Charan Kanoa, while other troops in LVT(A)s, which now mounted heavier caliber, short-barreled seventy-five millimeter guns, quickly advanced inland. Their objective was to seize and occupy 0-1, a low ridge roughly 1,500 yards inland which overlooked the landing beaches and Charan Kanoa, especially from the ridge's highest point, Mount Fina Susu.

After almost two weeks at sea, LST 19 and other LSTs in the convoy dropped anchor at Eniwetok Atoll in the Marshall Islands. Faster APAs and supply and fire support ships joined them for the final six day voyage to Saipan. In this period the inspections, briefings, and rebriefings intensified. The card games and bull sessions continued, but men now spoke in quieter tones, wrote letters to families and loved ones, and dwelled more in their private thoughts. Ayresie's machine gunners cleaned and oiled their weapons. Bob Avery and Ski carefully checked their belted 30.06 ammunition round by round to prevent any jamming of their Brownings in combat.

At dawn on June 15, 1944, LST 19 stood ten miles off Charan Kanoa. As H hour approached, the ship slowly moved shoreward, pausing three miles off Blue Beaches One and Two. Inside its well deck, engines of LVTs rumbled to life and filled the still air with exhaust fumes. On order, Ayresie and his machine gun squad, sweating in their sage green utilities, camouflage-covered helmets, boondockers, and leggings, clambered with their machine gun, ammunition, and personal weapons aboard their assigned LVT.

Within the LST's well deck, occasional shouted commands could be heard above the din of LVT engines. Minutes later, daylight flooded the well deck as the ship's massive steel bow doors opened. One by one the loaded LVTs lurched forward with their tracks clattering on the steel well deck, plunged down the bow ramp through the opened bow doors, dipped into the sea, leveled, and proceeded toward their line of departure.

The contrast for BLT 3/23 between Operation Forager and Operation Flintlock at Roi Island was enormous. Company I was no longer landing to reinforce and support Marines who had led the assault and cleared the enemy beaches. Ayresie, his squad, and the other Marines of BLT 3/23 were now in the initial assault waves, approaching a well-defended and artillery-torn beach and a lengthy and difficult battle. BLT 3/23 was on the tip of the spear thrusting into Japan's inner defenses.

The assault waves passed through battleships, cruisers, and destroyers sending salvo after salvo overhead onto Saipan's beaches and inland targets. LCIs approached the shore, launching hundreds of 4.5 inch rockets toward suspected enemy positions. These were followed by LVT(A)s firing their seventy-five millimeter guns. During carefully planned intervals between the fusillades of naval gunfire, US Navy fighters and torpedo planes bombed and fired 5-inch rockets and strafed the beaches, now obscured by the ferocity and intensity of the supporting fires.

Marines who lifted their heads to glance shoreward often risked and occasionally lost their lives in doing so. Nevertheless, as the LVT carrying Ayresie's squad passed beyond the fringing reef off Blue Beach One, Tom Savery glanced quickly over the side and noticed several small flag markers positioned near the reef and in the inner lagoon toward the shoreline. Tom's first thought was that the markers were intended to guide the LVTs in their assault waves toward shore. He was mistaken. The markers had been placed by the Japanese to aid gunners on Afetna Point just to the north, and other Japanese in positions on high ground inland who had preregistered their mortars and artillery on specific target areas marked by the flags. As the LVTs began to enter the zone of the flag markers, these enemy weapons commenced a heavy barrage, dropping their shells among the approaching assault waves. Near misses sent plumes of sea water into the air, but some shells struck home, destroying the landing crafts and badly wounding or killing their crews and the Marines crouching below their gunwales.

Just inland from Blue Beach One, the devastated town of Charan Kanoa could be seen dimly through swirling dust and smoke. Few buildings were undamaged, but a tall masonry smokestack remained intact looming above the ruins of Charan Kanoa's sugar mill. As the LVT carrying Ayresie's squad neared the shore, the furious Japanese artillery and mortar fire continued. Exploding artillery and mortar shells crashed closely about disembarking Marines. On every hand, men fell dead or wounded, while calls of "Corpsman" rang out.

As their LVT ground to a halt just inland from Blue Beach One, Ayresie's squad climbed over its sides, dropped to the sand, and hurried forward with their Browning heavy and its ammunition. They soon reached a small building that remained partially intact despite the heavy and accurate shelling. There, they paused briefly as I Company's commanding officer began to reorganize and coordinate with other units assigned to secure the town. Ayresie, Tom, and Ski took up positions inside the battered building which afforded observation to the front and flanks and some protection from small arms fire. Bob Avery, carrying ammunition for the squad's Brownings, sheltered just outside in a large shell hole.

Ayresie's squad and other troops in the nearby assault waves were unaware that they were under close observation from above. An intrepid Japanese observer had concealed himself inside the top of the Charan Kanoa sugar mill's tall smokestack, and now looked down on Marine positions to call in artillery and mortar fire. This fact was not discovered or even suspected by the attacking Marines for days. All they knew was that they were being hit by accurate and intense fire wherever they moved.

Blue Beach is to the right or south of the pier, with Charan Kanoa's ruined sugar mill inland. The body of water inland from Charan Kanoa is Lake Susupe, with the O-1 ridge and Mount Fina Susu just beyond. Sunlit Hill 500 looms in the distance.

Mere minutes after most of the squad had entered the small building and taken up their positions, Japanese mortar rounds plunged through the remnants of the structure's roof and exploded on impact. Tom Savery, realizing that he was wounded by shrapnel that struck his leg and foot, called out, "Ayresie, I'm hit."

No corpsmen were in the immediate area. Ayresie examined and bandaged Tom's most serious wounds with the dressing in his individual first aid kit. His number one gunner could no longer walk, and could only hobble slowly with assistance. Soon, orders to advance inland were received, and Ayresie's squad prepared to move. Tom Savery had no choice but to wait with his carbine until stretcher bearers or a corpsman could assist him to an aid station. Ayresie and the rest of his squad had no choice but to move forward in the attack, leaving Tom in the rough shelter.

The uninjured members of Ayresie's squad shouldered their burdens and moved outside to collect their ammunition bearer. To their horror and dismay, Bob Avery lay dead in his improvised foxhole. The handsome Marine had been struck squarely in the head by an unexploded Japanese mortar shell, which lay next to his body. Although the dud mortar round had not detonated, its impact at the terminus of its descending trajectory had killed him instantly.

In a matter of seconds, Ayresie had lost two of his closest buddies and two key members of his machine gun squad.

Marines are trained to continue their attack and complete their mission at all costs, despite their buddies' becoming casualties. As Japanese artillery and mortar fire continued to fall, the remaining squad members quickly marked the location of Bob's body, redistributed his 250-round containers of ammunition, and leaving the immobile Tom Savery inside his improvised shelter, moved forward.

Heavy, accurate artillery and mortar fire continued unabated throughout the afternoon and evening of June 15. In the meantime, assault units of the Second and Fourth Divisions had been unable to tie in their lines for the night. As the result of strong northerly currents, and heavy concentrations of Japanese fire that engaged the Second Division's LVTs from Afetna Point on their approach to the Green Beaches, the Second Division's troops had been forced to land further north than planned. The result was a substantial gap between the Second Division to the north and the Fourth Division to the south.

Some units of 3/23 aboard armored LVTs had reached the 0-1 line on Mount Fina Susu before being halted by heavy mortar and artillery fire. Those units were forced to withdraw to the rear or west, short of the 0-1 line, where BLT 1/23 relieved 3/23. The Marines of 3/23 assembled in the rear and took up positions to protect or "refuse" the Fourth Division's left flank, where Second Division troops remained to the north and were unable to close the gap.

In the early morning darkness of June 16, a Japanese counterattack struck squarely at the left flank of the Fourth Division held by Ayresie's Company I and Company K of 3/23. The apparent Japanese objectives were to seize the pier at Charan Kanoa and wreak havoc on the beachhead. The riflemen and machine gunners of I and K Companies repelled this attack, killing some 200 Japanese.

By 1000 hours on June 16, contact between the Second Division's Eighth Marines and 3/23 had been established on the beach at the Charan Kanoa Pier. The Eighth Marines prepared to move forward. At 1245, BLTs 1/23 and 2/23 resumed their attack to 0-1, with 3/23 in reserve.

As Ayresie's squad moved forward with I Company through the continuing bombardment toward 0-1, and participated in mopping up isolated pockets of Japanese that had been bypassed, shrapnel from an exploding Japanese mortar round struck him in his left arm and shoulder. The wounds did not impede his movements for long. The tough corporal was examined and bandaged at the closest aid station, refused evacuation, and quickly rejoined his machine gun squad.

By late afternoon of June 16, Regimented Combat Team Twenty-Three, called "RCT-23," had seized at great cost its assigned beachhead, secured the town of Charan Kanoa, and had fought to and secured 0-1 in its assigned sector. By this time, fully half of Company I had been killed or wounded, and these severe losses were typical of those suffered by the entire Third Battalion. For this reason, Companies I, K, L, and Headquarters Company of the Third Battalion were merged into two separate "composite" companies, which were attached to 2/23.

As nightfall of June 16 approached on the slopes of 0-1, Ayresie's squad placed their machine guns to aid in repelling an anticipated Japanese counterattack. Fortunately for the depleted squad the expected Japanese counterattack did not occur in their sector. To the north, however, the Japanese launched several probing attacks against the lines of the Second Division. These were followed in the early dawn hours of June 17 by a strong night attack led by over forty tanks mounting thirty-seven and forty-seven millimeter guns. The Marines of the Second Division's BLTs 1/6 and 2/2 effectively repelled the attack. Most of the Japanese tanks sent against the Second Division were destroyed by a combination of American Sherman medium tanks, Marine artillery, and thirty-seven millimeter anti-tank guns. Several teams armed with 2.36 millimeter bazookas, which were effective against the thin armor of Japanese tanks, contributed to their destruction. Marine machine gunners and riflemen cut down Japanese troops riding on or advancing with their tanks. Marine losses were not insignificant, but the casualties inflicted on the enemy were far greater. In this attack, the Japanese lost most of their tanks on Saipan to the combined Marine fires.

The Second Division's right flank units and the Fourth Division's left flank units had closed the gap separating them at Charan Kanoa on June 16. However, for several days the two divisions found it extremely difficult to maintain contact in their eastward advance as the result of a combination of certain terrain features inland, and Japanese troops taking skilled advantage of them.

As the Second and Fourth Divisions attacked inland, Lake Susupe, a sizable lake with swamps and marshes to its north and south, sat astride the boundary between the two divisions. The lake presented a half-mile wide water obstacle directly in the path of the Marines' advance. Its swamps and marshes, in which Japanese machine gunners and riflemen were concealed, further extended this barrier.

Second Division Marines came under fire from hidden Japanese riflemen and machine gunners hidden in the lake's northern marshes as they struggled forward, some sinking to their knees into the muck. Maintaining contact with the Fourth Division Marines to the right, or south, was impossible in this area, both tactically and physically, and the gap between the divisions reopened as soon as the Marines' eastern advance moved beyond Charan Kanoa.

The 0-1 ridge and Mount Fina Susu lay just to the east of Lake Susupe and its marshes. On and around the 0-1 line was a large coconut grove in which the Japanese had prepared concealed positions manned by hundreds of troops, armed with light howitzers, heavy and light mortars, anti-tank guns, and machine guns. From these strong positions, the Japanese inflicted heavy casualties on the Eighth Marines attacking eastward from the northwest, and on the Twenty-Third Marines, augmented by BLT 3/24, attacking eastward from the southwest. Both units were hampered in their ability to employ supporting naval gunfire or Marine artillery by their close proximity on either side of the grove and the division boundary.

Not until D+5, June 20, was the coconut grove reduced and firm contact between the two divisions restored.

The Great Marianas Turkey Shoot

On June 17, as Company I and the Fourth Division continued to fight eastward across Saipan, events well to the west of the expanding Marine beachhead began to unfold, with critical implications for the Americans and Japanese locked in combat ashore.

Japanese strategists long had been aware that the loss of Saipan would place their empire in an untenable position. Their land-based strategy to avoid this outcome consisted of an effort to halt the invading American Marines with a strong shoreline defense, and quickly overrun the vulnerable survivors by tank-led counterattacks.

This strategy was augmented by a naval plan. The Japanese fleet, still a formidable force, planned to defeat the American carriers, battleships, and transports mounting the Marianas invasion in a decisive sea engagement, supported by aircraft from Japan's surviving carriers and from its remaining airbases in the central Pacific. By defeating the American fleet and stranding Marines on Saipan without supplies, ammunition, and reinforcements, Japan hoped to deal a crushing blow to America's effort to take the Marianas.

By June 17, 1944, the third day of Operation Forager, American submarines had sighted and reported ships of the Japanese combined fleet advancing from the Philippine Islands eastward toward the Marianas. Operation "A-Go," Japan's effort to defeat the American advance in the Pacific, was underway.

On the same day, Admiral Spruance ordered the fast carriers of Admiral Mitscher's Task Force Fifty-Eight, part of the US Fifth Fleet, to meet the Japanese fleet, while other elements remained in a position west of Saipan to block any Japanese ships that might slip past Mitscher's carriers. Vice Admiral Turner, Naval Commander of the Northern Attack Force, withdrew his amphibious fleet and transports eastward a sufficient distance to isolate then from direct attack by the advancing Japanese fleet, protect reserve troops still embarked, and preserve ammunition, food, and supplies vital to the Marines fighting on Saipan.

Several anxious days passed ashore as American and Japanese aircraft met and engaged in air-to-air combat hundreds of miles away. Fortunately for the United States, this battle, officially named the First Battle of the Philippine Sea, was such a resounding American victory that it came to be known among exuberant American pilots as the Great Marianas Turkey Shoot.

On June 19, 1944, the first day of the conflict, the Japanese strike force lost three-quarters of its 430 carrier aircraft with their pilots and crews at a cost of thirty American carrier aircraft. In addition, two Japanese aircraft carriers were sunk by American submarines.

On the following day, determined pilots and crews from Mitscher's carriers pursued the remaining Japanese fleet as it withdrew toward the northwest to refuel. The American pilots' fuel supplies ran dangerously low, despite their carriers following at full speed to reduce the distance for the returning aircraft. As daylight waned, the American pilots caught the fleeing Japanese, sank a third carrier, and shot down sixty-five more Japanese planes while losing twenty planes to enemy fire.

Their mission accomplished, the surviving pilots banked and turned toward their carriers, still many miles away. Even if the pilots were able to locate and reach their assigned carriers with their remaining fuel, landing on their flight decks at night would be difficult and hazardous.

Task Force Fifty-Eight had not accurately located the Japanese fleet until the late afternoon of June 20. As a result, the American pilots were unable to launch their planes until late afternoon. Admiral Mitscher had ordered the attack to proceed knowing that pursuit of the Japanese fleet would severely challenge the aircrafts' operational range. In so doing, the Admiral placed the important mission's accomplishment above the personal welfare of his pilots, as combat commanders must do.

Now, as the pilots nursed their planes home toward their carriers in darkness, Mitscher made yet another bold command decision. Belaying the normal darkening of ships at nighttime in combat areas to avoid attack by Japanese submarines, the admiral ordered his carriers to fully illuminate their flight decks, and to turn their powerful searchlights aloft as beacons to guide his pilots home. Spontaneous and defiant cheers arose from American flight deck crews and from pilots who were not assigned to the day's mission.

Eighty American aircraft were lost as they ran short of fuel and ditched in the Pacific. Forty-nine pilots or crew members were lost at sea, but others were rescued by the end of the following day.

By eliminating most of Japan's trained and experienced naval aviators, this one-sided battle severely decimated Japanese naval aviation for the balance of World War II. In the near term, it had protected the Saipan invasion force, assured continuing supplies for Operation Forager, and doomed the hopes of the defenders of Saipan and Tinian for reinforcement or further naval and air support.

The Battle Ashore Continues

Operation Forager's original operation plan called for securing southern Saipan and capturing Aslito Air Field near its southern coast. Meanwhile, the Fourth Division was to advance and secure Saipan's eastern coast as far north as Magicienne Bay. With the Second Division as a "hinge" holding fast on the left or west, the Fourth Division would pivot and swing to the north. After coming on line, the two adjacent Marine divisions would attack northward to take the balance of the island. This plan required that the Fourth Division, and the Twenty-Third and Twenty-Fifth Marines in particular, attack quickly eastward across Saipan to Magicienne Bay and Saipan's east coast.

The plan, and Operation Forager's schedule, did not account for the many and varied difficulties presented by Japanese machine gunners and snipers lying hidden in dense cane fields and jungles, or Japanese mortars and artillery in Saipan's mountains, caves, and crevices, all bringing fire to bear against Marines attacking over very difficult terrain. Every advance, particularly in the early days of the Saipan operation, came at a heavy cost in Americans killed or wounded.

Confronted on the night of June 16 by heavy Marine casualties suffered during the first two days of Operation Forager, and by the perceived need for the transports and supply ships to deploy to the east for protection, General Holland Smith ordered the US Army's Twenty-Seventh Division to land in support of his two Marine divisions.

Two of the Twenty-Seventh Division's regiments landed on the night of June 16 and the morning of June 17. One of the army regiments was ordered to capture Aslito Airfield. By the night of June 18, the airfield had been captured, and army troops were attempting to eliminate resistance along Saipan's south coast. The other army regiment remained in position ashore as the Northern Landing Force Reserve. In the meantime, elements of the Twenty-Fourth Marines had reached the east coast of Saipan in their assigned sector.

On the morning of D plus 2, June 17, as BLT 1/23 and 2/23 advanced beyond the ridge designated 0-1 and turned left toward the northeast, heavy machine gun and mortar fire erupted from the coconut grove to their north, inflicting heavy casualties on 1/23, and pinning its surviving Marines down. BLT 2/23 on the right also had encountered strong resistance halting its advance just 300 yards beyond 0-1.

BLT 1/23's survivors of the heavy fire from the coconut grove withdrew with their wounded to the 0-1 ridge. Following hasty reorganization and a brief artillery preparation, 1/23 resumed its attack to the northeast at 1500 hours. The Marine artillery preparation, carefully limited to avoid the Second Marine Division's troops beyond the coconut grove to the north, had little, if any, effect. The advancing Marines on 1/23 again came under heavy Japanese mortar and machine gun fire from the grove which stalled their advance after a gain of only 200 yards.

By this time, 2/23 on the right had advanced another 200 yards, creating a gap of several hundred yards between the two combat teams. 3/23 advanced and occupied this gap, creating a tied-in defense supported by Ayresie's and other units' machine guns. After darkness on June 17, BLT 3/24 relieved 2/23 in its sector of the defense line. To the north, the gap between the Second and Fourth Marine Divisions formed by Japanese holding the coconut grove remained.

On the morning of June 18, BLT 3/24 passed through 1/23 and joined 2/23, and elements of 3/23 including I Company, to continue the northeastward advance. These attacking units were again stymied by fire from the coconut grove after proceeding 200 yards. At this point, 1/23's Marines capable of combat joined Headquarters Company of 3/23 to form a composite company. Advancing to the left of the other stalled units, this combined group partially penetrated the grove but was unable to kill all of its tenacious Japanese defenders.

On the morning of June 19, patrols probing to the northeast again reported machine gun and rifle fire from the coconut grove and from Hill 500, a well defended position directly in the path of the Twenty-Third Marines' advance to the northeast. The composite unit comprised of 1/23 and Headquarters Company of 3/23 attacked the coconut grove again and finally reduced the stubborn, well-defended position by evening. On the right, following another artillery preparation, 2/23, with I Company's rifle platoons and Ayresie's machine gun squad attached, advanced and seized what previously had been designated as 0-2, the second day's objective.

When mopping up of the coconut grove by 1/23 was completed in the late hours of June 20, several concealed pill boxes, caves, and individual rifle pits or "spider holes" were discovered among the palm trees and thick foliage. These were destroyed by explosive charges or sealed. The bodies of some twenty-five enemy dead were found above ground. Numerous mortars, heavy and light machine guns, howitzers, and other heavy weapons also were found and destroyed.

By June 20, the rifle companies and machine gun squads of 3/23, and of the other landing teams of the Twenty-Third Marines, were badly in need of rest, resupply, and whatever replacements were available. On that day, the entire Twenty-Third Marine Regiment was ordered into Fourth Division Reserve. BLT 3/23 was ordered to an assembly area to reorganize into its original but still understrength three rifle companies.

The Twenty-Fifth Marines relieved the Twenty-Third Regiment, now in division reserve. On June 20, 3/25 attacked following an artillery barrage through a well-placed smoke-screen to seize and occupy Hill 500. After the hill was secured, Marines of 3/25 discovered forty-four Japanese bodies, and spent the remainder of the day burning out and sealing caves holding an undetermined number of Japanese defenders who refused to emerge to fight or surrender.

By the evening of June 21, all of southern Saipan, except for pockets of Japanese resistance near Nafutan Point and Aslito Airfield, was in American hands. Capturing this portion of the island had cost over 6,000 Marine casualties. On that evening, General Holland Smith issued orders for the Second and Fourth Marine Divisions to complete their pivot to the north, where some 15,000 of General Saito's determined troops remained to confront their advance.

On the morning of June 22, the Second Division's Sixth Marines overran portions of Mount Tipo Pale just south of Mount Tapotchau, while the adjacent Eighth Marines attacked northward into the hills and ridges nearby.

The Fourth Division's Twenty-Fourth and Twenty-Fifth Marines attacked northward, while the Twenty-Third Marines followed in trace in reserve. The Twenty-Fifth Marines, attacking on the left against a series of four ridges with two companies abreast, immediately encountered strong Japanese resistance, and in the ensuing battle ninety Japanese were killed. Advancing north another 2,000 yards, the Twenty-Fifth Marines were halted by Japanese concealed in caves on the fourth ridge and in the thick growth at its base. On the right, the Twenty-Fourth Marines advanced northward through gullies and broken ground along the eastern shores of Magicienne Bay.

A General Is Relieved of His Command

The increasingly difficult terrain features and undergrowth, heavy Marine casualties, stiff resistance by the Japanese, and the need to attack and secure the Kagman Peninsula jutting seaward two miles from Saipan's eastern shore, would have required the attacking Marine divisions to be spread dangerously thin. General Holland Smith now concluded that he had no choice but to fully commit most of his Northern Landing Force Reserve, the US Army's Twenty-Seventh Division, to the advance, leaving one battalion of the division to eliminate Japanese resistance near Saipan's southeast coast. On June 22, 1944, he ordered units of the Twenty-Seventh Division into the lines between the Second and Fourth Marine Divisions. The following day, the three divisions were to participate in a coordinated attack northward.

Unfortunately, a pattern of unduly slow, if not outright hesitant response of the army's Twenty-Seventh Division to General Holland Smith's orders, and its soldiers' failure to keep pace with advancing Marine units, met with serious displeasure on the part of the Northern Landing Force commander.

On the morning of June 23, the 106th and 165th Army Infantry Regiments had been ordered to proceed to the line of departure for the day's attack. Unfortunately, the two army regiments became confused and disorganized in their approach march to the line of departure and were not in position when the attack had been ordered to commence or "jump off." As a result, the attack of the 106th Regiment on the left was delayed almost an hour after the army's 165th Regiment attacked on the right. These problems also forced the attacking Marine units to pause in their advance, delaying and disrupting the entire attack to the north.

When the army units finally commenced their attack between the Second and Fourth Marine Divisions, they were entering an exposed and well-defended area extending northward over a relatively flat plateau between concealed Japanese positions in Mount Tapotchau eastern cliffs and slopes to the left, and other commanding positions on a series of hills forming an irregular ridge to the right. At the southern entrance of this plateau, Japanese in caves brought heavy fire to bear. This particular gateway position came to be called "Hell's Pocket" by the soldiers. The plateau itself, and the irregular ridge to the east, they named "Death Valley" and "Purple Heart Ridge," respectively.

The attacking army units failed to reduce Hell's Pocket or to advance significantly into Death Valley on June 23. Although these terrain features in the Twenty-Seventh Division's zone presented difficult obstacles, the same was true of all Marine and army units participating in the Saipan campaign.

When the Twenty-Seventh Division's regiments failed to advance on June 23, Marine General Holland Smith spoke to Army General Sanford Jarman, overall commander of the entire US Army garrison on Saipan. In "Howlin' Mad's" usual plainspoken manner, he informed General Jarman that he felt the Twenty-Seventh Army Division was not doing its part in the advance. Holland Smith asked Jarman if he would press the Twenty-Seventh Division's Commander, General Ralph Smith, to attack aggressively and to avoid exposing the interior flanks of the adjacent Marine divisions. General Jarman agreed to do so. In fact, General Ralph Smith apparently was in agreement at that point with Holland Smith's assessment, stating that his Regiments "had not performed well that day." He upbraided his regimental commanders and ordered them to move forward aggressively in the next day's attack..

On the morning of June 24, General Holland Smith's plan of attack called for the Second Marine Division to seize Saipan's capital city, Garapan, on the west coast, while other Second Division units continued their effort to take and occupy the crest of Mount Tapotchau. As the Twenty-Seventh Army Division advanced northward into Death Valley, the Fourth Marine Division, with the Twenty-Third Marines and I Company in the lead, was ordered to advance eastward onto the Kagman Peninsula.

All Marine units jumped off in their attacks as ordered, against strong Japanese resistance.

In the center, the army's 165th Regiment attempted to bypass Death Valley to the right over ground east of Purple Heart Ridge that previously had been cleared by the Twenty-Third Marines. However, the 165th Regiment failed to achieve any advance in its zone. The 106th Regiment jumped off as ordered, but again met resistance from Hell's Pocket and was thrown back to its original line of departure.

Holland Smith's patience was exhausted. With the approval of overall Task Force Commander Spruance, he relieved General Ralph Smith from command of the Twenty-Seventh Army Division. This action clearly was Holland Smith's right as commander of all expeditionary troops in Operation Forager, in addition to his assignment as the Northern Landing Force Commander. Nevertheless, the army's storm of protest resulting from this wartime decision was immediate, continued throughout the Pacific war, and lingers in some quarters to this day.

Some well-documented conclusions by US Army officers held that the relief of Ralph Smith was justified. One Army Regimental Commander in the Saipan campaign stated that his army troops, at or shortly after the time of General Ralph Smith's relief from command, were hesitant to respond to orders and "preferred to return to their previous positions" when confronted by sniper fire or other comparatively light resistance.

Continuing bitterness and resentment on the part of senior US Army officers ultimately resulted in Marine General Holland Smith's being barred from attending Japan's formal surrender aboard the battleship USS *Missouri* in Tokyo Bay. Such treatment of the general who commanded all troops in Operation Forager, and who afterward led all Marines in the Fleet Marine Force Pacific, including those who fought to victory on Iwo Jima, was a sad example of post-war political expediency. This needless, conciliatory gesture denied a respected Pacific commander the right to attend the surrender of his enemy, solely because of petulance over a decision in the heat of combat he was fully authorized to make.

Northward Through Saipan

The relief of General Ralph Smith did not alter the plan of attack on Saipan. Over the next six days, from June 25 through June 30, the Second Marine Division overcame stiff resistance on steep and challenging terrain by taking Mount Tipo Pale, captured Mount Tapotchau, and on the west coast was poised to assault Garapan. The Fourth Marine Division captured the Kagman Peninsula and continued its attack northward along the eastern portion of Saipan, fighting through the ravines and bluffs along the eastern coast.

In the center, the army's Twenty-Seventh Division, commanded by Major General Sanford Jarman, and subsequently by General George Griner, struggled forward. The division, whose pace of advance through Death Valley at one point allowed its front lines to sag over a mile behind the lines of the Fourth Marine Division on its right, had by June 30 reduced this sag to 500 yards. The Twenty-Seventh Division was able to cover this distance with patrols and by fire, and finally moved northward beyond Death Valley.

By July 1, the Second and Fourth Marine Divisions had suffered a combined 8,902 casualties since D-Day. The Twenty-Seventh Army Division had suffered 1,836 casualties, the majority of which were sustained in clearing Hell's Pocket, Death Valley, and Purple Heart Ridge.

On July 2, as the Second Marine Division continued to advance through Garapan and its adjacent high ground, the Marines of the Fourth Division, with the army's Twenty-Seventh Division to their left, continued their advance to the north. I Company and Ayresie's machine gunners participated in this advance, while other 3/23 units remained in the Twenty-Third Marines' regimental reserve.

On July 3, General Holland Smith ordered a change in the direction of the attack to the northeast, which was the true compass direction of the remaining Saipan land mass not yet in American hands. On July 4, the Second Marine Division was assigned to Northern Landing Force Reserve and ordered to remain in an area north of Garapan near Tanapag, while the Twenty-Seventh Army Division on the left, and the Fourth Marine Division on the right advanced to the northeast.

The Fourth Division's attack, with 3/23 in the lead, was ordered to jump off on July 5 after the assault units had adjusted their positions. Companies I and K of 3/23 then attacked a formidable and well-defended piece of high ground called Hill 721 and made some progress, but withdrew late in the day to allow an artillery preparation on the hill.

Although Ayresie's machine gun squad had suffered no further losses since D-Day, 3/23 again was operating at only 50 percent combat efficiency. BLT 1/23 now passed through 3/23, and following the planned artillery barrage on Hill 721, resumed the attack. Fortunately, the enemy had withdrawn from Hill 721 during the night, and 1/23 occupied this objective against little or no resistance.

The Fourth Marine Division's July 5 advance on the right again resulted in the army's Twenty-Seventh Division's falling behind on its left. General Holland Smith therefore ordered the Twenty-Seventh Division to change its direction of attack from northeast to north, and ordered the left flank of the Fourth Division to the northwest. The operation plan now called for the Twenty-Seventh Division and Fourth Marine Division to attack and seize the west coast of Saipan above the Village of Makunsha. Thereafter, the entire remaining northern portion of Saipan would be attacked and secured by the Fourth Marine Division, with the Second Division's BLT 2/2 attached. The army's Twenty-Seventh Division was ordered to remain on Saipan's western coast, and to patrol and reduce Japanese resistance in an area extending northward from Tanapag to the village of Makunsha.

The Gyokusai—Banzai!

By July 6, Japanese General Saito had repeatedly moved his headquarters and the Japanese lines of defense northward as he was pressed continuously from the south by the Americans. The ailing general now sheltered in a small, cramped cave in Paradise Valley, a mere quarter mile below the Fourth Division Marines' position on high ground in Saipan's central mountains. Fourth Division Marines had named a prominent portion of this high ground "Prudential Hill" for its resemblance to the Gibraltar trademark held by the American insurance company of that name.

General Saito realized that he had failed in the duty assigned to him by his emperor to defeat the Americans and preserve Saipan as a key strong point in Japan's inner ring of defense. His troops had fought fiercely without hope of reinforcements or resupply. Now diminished to a force of some five thousand to seven thousand men, they awaited his orders.

Concluding that "whether we attack or whether we stay where we are, there is only death," Saito sent a message to his surviving officers, praising the efforts of his troops against the "barbarous American devils." Saito further exhorted his troops to "exalt true Japanese manhood," and assuage the bitterness of defeat with a final banzai attack in which each soldier was to take seven American lives before sacrificing his own. The general pledged to leave his bones on Saipan as a "bulwark of the Pacific." However, General Saito would neither lead nor participate in the attack. Instead, the Japanese commander, along with the naval commander on Saipan, Admiral Nagumo Chuichi, would commit ritual suicide after Saito's final attack order was given.

Holland Smith had anticipated such an attack by Saipan's remaining Japanese. On July 6, he visited Army Major General Griner, cautioned him to be on the alert for an attack from the north, and instructed him to be sure his defenses were strongly tied in for the evening.

Before dawn on July 7 thousands of Japanese soldiers, both sound and walking wounded, and constituting most of Saipan's remaining defense garrison, assembled near Makunsha north of the US Army's 105th regiment. Many understood, accurately or inaccurately, that Saito's orders had originated directly from their emperor. This command by their divine emperor would constitute the banzai attack a "Gyokusai," further inspiring them to battle as if that were necessary.

The fanatical attack had no clear-cut tactical objective other than to inflict maximum casualties on the Americans. Some Japanese were armed with mortars, machine guns, and rifles. Others improvised crude lances by tying knives to bamboo poles. All apparently were well supplied with sake. A few Japanese tanks accompanied the soldiers.

On command, these massed troops swarmed southward from Makunsha down the Saipan's western coastal plain directly into the 105th Regiment's First and Second Battalions. Unfortunately, these two battalions had failed to close a substantial gap of some three to four hundred yards between their lines at the end of the day's advance. This gap had been discovered by probing Japanese patrols.

The attacking Japanese rushed against the 105th Regiment's First and Second Battalions like a human tsunami, and swarmed through the gap left between them.

Although some soldiers broke and ran, others fought bravely. US Army Lieutenant Colonel William O'Brien, Commanding Officer of First Battalion, 105th Regiment, stood his ground, leading and encouraging his troops. After exhausting his .45 pistol's ammunition, he climbed aboard a Jeep and fired its mounted machine gun until he fell. Colonel O'Brien's body was found surrounded by numerous Japanese soldiers slain by his efforts. He deserved and was awarded a posthumous Congressional Medal of Honor.

Despite the efforts of Lieutenant Colonel O'Brien and others, the soldiers were completely overrun by the mass of Japanese. Unable to halt or even slow the fanatical horde, some soldiers hurried along with their attackers, firing as they moved, like drovers keeping pace with a stampeding herd of cattle. Eventually, surviving soldiers drew up in pockets of resistance in and around Tanapag and defended themselves as best they could.

Fourth Division Marines on Prudential Hill to the east overlooked this mass attack at a distance. Some Marine mortar sections lobbed shells into the swarm of Japanese, and machine gunners attempted to bring long-range plunging fire to bear. Neither of these efforts could effectively blunt the fast-moving attack.

Some 1,000 yards to the south of the original positions held by the army's 105th Regiment, two artillery battalions of the Tenth Marines had moved into position to support by fire the planned northward advance by the Fourth Marine Division. As the attack surged southward, hundreds of attacking Japanese with tanks in support fell upon the 105 millimeter howitzer positions of H Battery, Tenth Marines. The Marine cannoneers lowered their muzzles and fired short-fused rounds at the attacking Japanese, some as close as fifty yards in front of their positions. One Howitzer was swung to the rear by its crew to destroy a Japanese tank.

The Marines fought with their artillery pieces, and then with their individual weapons until so many were killed that the survivors were forced to withdraw southward to a more tenable position. There, they formed a perimeter and resisted the attack with whatever weapons and ammunition remained or could be salvaged.

By midday of July 7, the ranks of the attacking Japanese had been substantially thinned by the surviving soldiers and Marine artillerymen, and the banzai attack dwindled to a few isolated pockets of Japanese. Several now began to commit suicide. By the early evening, most of the ground lost to the attackers had been regained.

This banzai attack and its immediate aftermath, in which the Japanese lost between 2,000 and 4,000 troops, also claimed the lives of over 400 soldiers, and 45 Marines of the Third Battalion, Tenth Marines. The effort ordered by General Saito added significantly to American casualties, but broke the back of organized Japanese resistance on Saipan.

The Battle Concludes

The Fourth Marine Division, with the Second Division's 2/2 attached, now shouldered the full responsibility of capturing the remaining northern portion of Saipan.

On the afternoon of July 6, hours before the Japanese banzai attack, BLTs 1/23 and 2/23 had commenced their advance to Saipan's west coast by descending the steep slopes of Prudential Hill. As the Marines moved cautiously downhill, they came under heavy machine gun fire from Japanese in concealed caves in the precipitous slopes above them. The advancing units were forced to retrace their steps to the summit and tie in their defenses for the night.

The following day 1/23 and 2/23 resumed the task of eliminating the Japanese occupying caves in and below the steep cliff line. Their objective was to establish a line of departure on the coastal plain for the next day's western advance to the sea. Resistance again was strong, and the Marines were further hampered by Japanese mines blocking access by tanks attempting to support their cave-clearing operation. At the end of the day, the Marines had inflicted casualties reducing the number of Japanese in these redoubts, but again had to withdraw to the summit of Prudential Hill for the night. The day's attempt had not been a complete loss. Halftracks mounting seventy-five millimeter guns and Marine machine gunners on and near Prudential Hill observed groups of Japanese survivors of the previous night's Gyokusai as they withdrew to the north along the western coast. The Japanese came within range of these weapons, were taken under fire, and suffered substantial casualties.

On July 8, trucks mounting rocket launchers were lowered with cables down the slopes of Prudential Hill. Now, occupying positions on the lower ground, the rocket launchers, joined by LCI rocket boats offshore, bombarded the Japanese cave positions among the slopes and cliffs above. With this support, BLTs 1/23 and 2/23 were able to clear the cave positions and complete their advance down the slopes of Prudential Hill. As the teams crossed the level ground below, Ayresie and other machine gunners, and the riflemen and mortarmen of 3/23, supported their advance from positions on the high ground. By noon, the Twenty-Third Marines had reached Saipan's western coast north of Makunsha.

On July 9, the entire Twenty-Third Marine Regiment was assigned to Fourth Division Reserve and ordered to mop up isolated Japanese along Saipan's western shore. By the late afternoon of July 9, BLTs 2/2, 3/24, and 3/25, attacking against vastly diminished and disorganized Japanese resistance, had reached and occupied the entirety of Saipan's northern coast, completing the capture of Saipan.

By July 15, the Twenty-Third Marines' patrolling and mopping up efforts had eliminated virtually all Japanese on or near the west coast that were inclined to show themselves. On that day, Ayresie's regiment was relocated south to an assembly area near Charan Kanoa for reorganization, rehabilitation, and to prepare for further operations. There the Marines rested, ate, and replaced their worn boondockers, rotted socks, and torn and shredded utilities, none of which had been washed, changed, or replaced during a full month of heavy fighting over Saipan's invasion beaches and rough terrain. Ayresie's squad and the other machine gun crews of the Twenty-Third Marines cleaned, adjusted, and test fired their weapons.

The Twenty-Third Marines were spared a harrowing experience at Saipan's northern coast, which was witnessed first-hand by other Marines of the Fourth Division. When the invasion of Saipan commenced on June 15, 1944, thousands of Japanese civilians, most of whom had been employed in the sugar cane industry, still remained on the island. These Japanese had withdrawn northward with their troops, who repeatedly assured them that if they fell into Marine hands, they and their families would suffer torture, murder, and rape by the American "barbarians."

These allegations by Japanese soldiers were, of course, untrue. Marine interpreters, with the assistance of captured

Japanese soldiers or civilians, spoke through loudspeakers and bullhorns, and repeatedly urged surviving Japanese, both soldiers and civilians, to surrender and receive humane treatment. Some responded to these pleas. However, many Japanese civilians attempting to approach the American lines in response to these entreaties were killed by their own soldiers. Hundreds of other civilians joined their families and leapt to their deaths off the precipitous cliffs of "Suicide Hill," or died by leaping from the high cliffs of Saipan's northern coast onto the rocks below. Many Japanese soldiers and civilians simply swam into the ocean and deliberately drowned. Even combat-hardened Marines were shaken as they observed this needless orgy of self-destruction.

The conquest of Saipan was a major strategic American victory. Most Japanese leaders felt that Saipan's loss inevitably would lead to Japan's defeat in World War II. General Saito is reported to have written, "The fate of the Empire will be decided in this one action." Following the Japanese defeat, Fleet Admiral Osami Nagano, the naval advisor to Emperor Hirohito, lamented, "When we lost Saipan, Hell is on us."

Immediately after Saipan fell, Japanese Premier Hideki Tojo, who long had pressed and encouraged Japan's war on the United States, was relieved as head of the Japanese Army. On July 18, 1944, Tojo resigned as premier with his entire wartime cabinet.

Among the approximately 25,000 Japanese killed on Saipan was Vice Admiral Nagumo, who committed ritual suicide with General Saito. Nagumo had led Japan's December 7, 1941, sneak attack on Pearl Harbor.

The United States Marines of the Second and Fourth Divisions, with the assistance of the soldiers of the US Army's Twenty-Seventh Division, had captured Saipan and destroyed its garrison, including the highest ranked Japanese naval and army commanders on Saipan. In his book *Coral and Brass*, General Holland Smith stated that the effect of the American conquest and occupation of Saipan was equivalent to the hypothetical effect on the United States had the Japanese, following their December 7, 1941, aerial attack on Pearl Harbor, landed on Oahu, taken the entire island, and killed all American military personnel, including Admiral Nimitz and all senior army and navy commanders. The general's comparison is difficult to challenge.

Despite expressions of pessimism by some Japanese military leaders following the loss of Saipan, Emperor Hirohito and other senior Japanese military officers resolved to continue fighting until the bitter end. American commanders expected nothing less.

Ayresie and the other Marines of the Second and Fourth Divisions now prepared for another task. To the immediate south of Saipan lay Tinian, defended by some 9,000 Japanese troops. On July 21, 1944, the commanding officers of the Twenty-Third Marines' three infantry battalions boarded observation planes and conducted their own personal aerial reconnaissance of Tinian. Three days later, the Twenty-Fourth and Twenty-Fifth Marines would lead the Fourth Marine Division's assault on the island.

CHAPTER 8

TINIAN

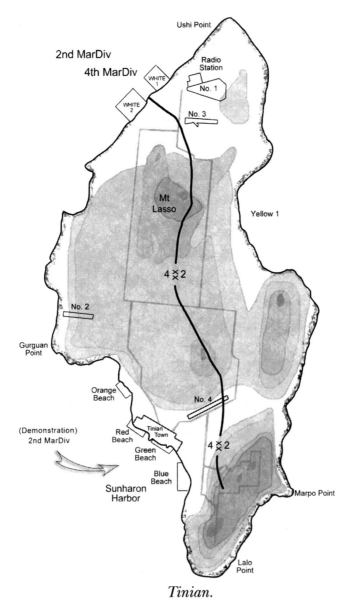

Ushi Point

2nd MarDiv
4th MarDiv

Radio
Station

WHITE
1

No. 1

WHITE
2

No. 3

Mt
Lasso

Yellow 1

4 ⚔ 2

No. 2

Gurguan
Point

Orange
Beach

No. 4

(Demonstration)
2nd MarDiv

Red
Beach

Tinian
Town

Green
Beach

4 ⚔ 2

Blue
Beach

Marpo Point

Sunharon
Harbor

Lalo
Point

Tinian.

The island of Tinian's level terrain, most of which was planted in sugar cane, was better suited for airfields than that of Saipan. Three Japanese airfields already were in operation on Tinian, with one more under construction as the battle for Saipan drew to a close.

For weeks, as Marine and US Army artillery units on Saipan were no longer needed to support the continuing northward advance, their guns had displaced to positions on Saipan's southern shore and engaged targets located on Tinian. Soon, bombardment of Tinian by aircraft and naval gunfire joined the artillery fire from Saipan.

Less than two weeks following their capture of Saipan, and after losing a significant percentage of their combat strength, Marines of the Fourth Division gathered in assembly areas near Charan Kanoa, and prepared to board LSTs which would carry them the short distance to the invasion beaches on Tinian.

Major General Harry Schmidt, now commanding the Northern Landing Force and the Fifth Amphibious Corps, and Rear Admiral Harry Hill, commanding the Northern Task Force, with the assistance of General Holland M. Smith, who now led the entire Fleet Marine Force Pacific, had developed a bold plan for the invasion of Tinian. An obvious choice of landing beaches for the American invasion would have focused upon the expansive shoreline at Tinian Town and Sunharon Harbor. Anticipating just such an attack, the Japanese commander of troops on Tinian, Colonel Keishi Ogata, had emplaced most of his heavy guns and artillery on the heights that commanded those sites, and positioned most of the 9,000 troops defending Tinian in or near that area.

Several hundred yards apart on Tinian's isolated northwest coast near Ushi Point were two very narrow beaches, one only sixty yards wide and the other one hundred yards wide. While these beaches, designated White One and White Two, presented an imposing tactical and logistical challenge, they were several miles north of the strongest Japanese concentrations of troops and artillery poised in anticipation of expected American landings near Tinian Town.

Before Saipan was officially declared secure, Marines and US Navy Underwater Demolition Team members were on Tinian's northwestern beaches to evaluate their suitability for getting the invading troops ashore and organized into a well-defended beachhead before the Japanese reacted in force. On the nights of July 10 and 11, two weeks before "J" day scheduled for July 24, 1944, "Recon" Marines from V Amphibious Corps' Reconnaissance Battalion, accompanied by Navy UDT "frogmen," landed in darkness from rubber boats. These specialists carefully studied White Beaches One and Two, and their surf conditions, approaches, and beach exits inland. The Recon Marines and UDT team reported that, while far narrower than any previous Pacific invasion site, White Beaches One and Two would permit the landing of LVTs on a narrow front, while LCMs and LCVPs could debark tanks, troops, and equipment outside the shallow reef only one hundred yards from shore. It would, of course, be mandatory that assault troops move inland as rapidly as possible and clear these narrow invasion beaches for succeeding waves. The guarded conclusion of US Navy and Marine commanders was that, given favorable weather and the element of surprise, a landing on the White Beaches was feasible. This conclusion eventually was approved by Admiral Richard Turner, commanding the Joint Expeditionary Force and Task Force Fifty-One.

To further enhance the element of surprise, the Second and Eighth Regiments of the Second Marine Division would conduct a feint landing at Tinian Town, conceived and planned to be more convincing than that conducted on D-Day at Saipan's Tanapeg Harbor.

On July 23, 1944, Ayresie and the surviving members of his machine gun squad moved seaward across the beach where they had landed under a torrent of Japanese mortar and artillery fire on June 15, and boarded LST 487 for the short ride to Tinian. There, anchored 3,000 yards off White Beaches One and Two, the Marines waited in rain and darkness for the dawn of July 24 and the outcome of their commanders' bold gamble.

At sunrise, Japanese gunners in and near Tinian Town awoke to the sight of American fire support ships offshore, which soon commenced a preinvasion bombardment. American aircraft also bombed and strafed targets ashore. Attack transports conspicuously lowered their LCVPs. Marines appeared to descend cargo nets, but their absence in the LCVPs went undetected. Navy coxswains soon gunned their landing craft toward shore without a visible troop cargo.

The Japanese immediately unleashed furious heavy weapons fire against the naval gunships and waves of assault craft. The LCVPs withdrew, paused to reform, and came on again in an apparent second effort to land in the face of renewed Japanese fire. Finally, several hundred yards from shore, the landing craft turned and made for their transports.

The ruse appeared to have convinced the Japanese that an invasion had been repulsed at the predicted landing beach. In fact, Japanese fire had caused significant casualties aboard the battleship *Colorado* and the destroyer *Norman Scott*. Colonel Ogata informed Tokyo that the American landing had been repulsed. A soldier in his unit wrote in his diary, "… maybe the enemy has retreated."

The hopes of Colonel Ogata and his young soldier were soon dashed. As the fraudulent diversion proceeded at Tinian Town, assault troops from the Twenty-Fourth and Twenty-Fifth Marines hurried ashore aboard their LVTs on White Beaches One and Two. Ayresie's Twenty-Third Marines was assigned to division reserve, and his squad remained for the moment aboard LST 487.

Only sporadic rifle and machine gun fire met the attacking Marines on White One, who quickly overcame the small detachment of defenders. On White Two, a larger defensive detachment manned two pillboxes, but they also were soon dispatched. All Marines then quickly cleared the beaches for other closely following LVTs and moved toward their assigned first day's objectives. The Twenty-Fourth Marines assumed defensive positions on the left or northern flank of the beach-head. Other units of the Twenty-Fourth Marines and assault units of the Twenty-Fifth Marines held the center.

Major General Clifton B. Cates, now commanding the Fourth Marine Division, soon decided that he should land his division reserve to support and strengthen the expanding beachhead held by his understrength assault units. By 1630 on J-Day, Ayresie's Company I and the entire Twenty-Third Marine regiment had come ashore on White Beach Two. BLT 2/23 occupied front line positions facing southward on the right or southern flank of the beachhead. BLT 1/23 dug in behind 2/23, while BLT 3/23 remained close at hand in a reserve defensive position. All hands were alerted that the Japanese were expected to attempt a strong counterattack consistent with their tactics on Saipan.

And soon they did. Within hours, Japanese commanders had learned of the landings on the White Beaches. Hundreds of their troops now marched north from the vicinity of Tinian Town and other sectors of the island where they had remained stationed awaiting orders to attack.

At 0200 on July 25, one unit of about 600 Japanese naval troops struck southward against the Twenty-Fourth Marines, holding the northern flank of the beachhead. These attack-ing Japanese were armed with rifles, hand grenades, and several machine guns salvaged from aircraft destroyed in the bombardment of Tinian. In the shifting light of Marine flares, the Japanese naval troops, many of whom wore white gloves rendering them more visible, were decimated by a combination of deadly canister rounds fired by crews manning thirty-seven millimeter anti-tank guns, by mortar fire, and by the machine gun and rifle fire of the Twenty-Fourth Marines. Over 400 of the attacking Japanese were killed outright in this attack.

In the center of the beachhead held by units from the Twenty-Fourth and Twenty-Fifth Marines, a well-armed and trained Japanese infantry unit attacked at 0230, exploiting a lightly manned gap between the two regiments. The Japanese achieved a temporary penetration that was soon repulsed by Marine riflemen and machine gunners supported by tanks, artillery, and mortars. Daylight revealed the bodies of some 500 Japanese who died attempting this breakthrough.

At 0330 on the right or southern flank of the beachhead, five Japanese tanks supported by artillery fire and infantry troops attacked northward against the line held by BLT 2/23. The Japanese tanks were quickly destroyed by bazookas and the thirty-seven millimeter anti-tank guns of 2/23, bolstered by those of BLT 3/23's weapons platoon. The Japanese continued to press their attack against the riflemen and machine gunners of 2/23 and the combined fires of thirty-seven millimeter anti-tank gunners firing deadly canister shells against the waves of attacking Japanese soldiers. One Twenty-Third Marine gunner described the grisly task of going forward during a lull in the fighting, and tossing aside the accumulation of Japanese bodies to reopen fields of fire for his crew's thirty-seven millimeter gun.

This attack from the south against the Twenty-Third Marines fared no better than those against the northern and center sectors of the beachhead.

Overall, some 1,200 Japanese troops lost their lives in the banzai attacks during the night of J-Day and early morning of J plus one. The dead included many of the best Japanese infantry troops committed to the counterattack. The attack certainly had cost Marine lives, including those of two decorated Twenty-Fifth Marine machine gunners who steadfastly remained at their forward machine gun positions and continued firing. These two Marines accounted for over 200 dead Japanese before they were overrun and killed. The disciplined and determined stand during the night of J-Day, in the words of FMF Pacific Commander Holland Smith in *Coral and Brass*, had "sealed the fate of Tinian."

On J plus 1, July 25, 1944, the Second Marine Division landed on the White Beaches, and swinging to the east and north, passed to the left of the Fourth Division. By the end of the day, the entire Marine beachhead had expanded. The Twenty-Fourth and Twenty-Fifth Marines, with the Second Division's Eighth Marines on their left, had advanced eastward halfway across the island securing two of Tinian's airfields. The Twenty-Third Marines had advanced 1,000 yards to the south along the western coast. For this advance, Ayresie's 3/23 and Company I had moved out of Fourth Division Reserve and joined the attack, which continued until the Twenty-Third Marines came on line with the Twenty-Fifth Marines on its left.

On July 26, the Second Marine Division completed its advance to Tinian's east coast and prepared to move southward. The Fourth Division's Twenty-Fifth Marines, having taken 400 foot high Mount Maga, advanced southward toward Mount Lasso, at 560 feet in altitude the highest point on Tinian. Fortunately, the Marines found that the Japanese had withdrawn southward, abandoning this formidable obstacle.

In less than three days, the Northern Landing Force had landed two Marine divisions over a combined 160 yards of shoreline, and had captured the northern third of Tinian.

The Second Marine Division on the left or east, and the Fourth Marine Division on the right or west, with much of their supporting armor and artillery now relocated from Saipan, and air support on call within minutes from Saipan's Aslito airfield, stood poised to continue their attack southward.

General Schmidt now decided upon a unique plan for attacking southward. By using what was described as "elbowing" tactics, one division with massed artillery and air support would make the day's main attack in its sector. The other division would commence its attack later against the objective in its area of responsibility. The following day, the missions of the two divisions would be reversed, with the main attack now occurring with full support in the sector of the division mounting the previous day's later attack.

Thus, on July 27, 1944, the Second Marine Division attacked in its eastern zone of responsibility with full artillery support, and rolled southward across cane fields and farm country.

Resistance was light, and the Second Division's two assault regiments reached the day's objective by early afternoon.

On the west, the Fourth Division's Twenty-Third Marines, with I and K Companies in the lead, jumped off in their attack and reached their day's objective in a single hour with no enemy resistance. The Twenty-Third Marines then sent patrols forward another 1,000 yards, found no trace of the enemy, and dug in for the evening. Ayresie's squad, hauling their weapons, ammunition, and water in two-wheeled carts during the rapid advance over level terrain, positioned their Brownings in the line, but no counterattack or attempts at infiltration occurred.

On July 28, Companies I and K again led 3/23's advance in the day's main attack southward along Tinian's west coast. Their assigned objective was reached by early afternoon. BLT 3/23 had advanced 7,000 yards southward, but not without I Company's meeting stiffened Japanese resistance consisting of machine gun and mortar fire from troops in a large coastal village. This resistance was overcome by I and K Companies with the aid of Sherman tanks.

Tinian's relatively level terrain in this area was well suited for use of tanks and LVT(A)s, enabling the advancing Marines to employ a coordinated armor and infantry tactic. Sherman tanks led the advance, followed closely by LVT(A)s and Marine infantry advancing in a line of skirmishers. The Sherman tanks and armored LVTs provided fire support with their seventy-five millimeter guns and coaxial machine guns, while infantry protected them from attacks by hidden or infiltrating Japanese. In this manner, the Marines attacked rapidly while remaining strongly protected against ambushes and pockets of resistance left by the Japanese.

At the end of the southward advance on July 28, the island of Tinian narrowed dramatically at its western coast by over a mile. This geographical feature resulted in all battalions of the Twenty-Third Marines being temporarily "pinched out" of the line of advance to the south and placed in Fourth Division Reserve.

By July 29, General Schmidt's elbowing plan of attack was no longer needed. The Japanese now appeared to be rapidly withdrawing toward a high plateau in the south without putting up strong resistance against the Marine advance. Therefore, both division commanders were authorized by General Schmidt to advance simultaneously and as rapidly as possible in their sectors. Some pockets of enemy resistance were met and either quickly overcome or contained and bypassed to be reduced later.

The Twenty-Third Marines, hurriedly displacing forward in Fourth Division Reserve, remained in close contact with the assault units of the Twenty-Fourth and Twenty-Fifth Regiments. By the night of July 29, the Twenty-Fourth and Twenty-Fifth Marines could see scattered lights of Tinian Town from their fighting holes.

On July 30, the advance of the Twenty-Fourth Marines approached Tinian Town. The town was found to have been almost completely destroyed by the American bombardment before the simulated landing on J-Day and appeared to be deserted by the Japanese. However, in nearby coastal caves, pockets of Japanese armed with machine guns and rifles had to be destroyed by flame tanks or sealed in their caves with demolitions.

Following their thorough search of Tinian Town, which disclosed the presence of a single Japanese soldier, the Twenty-Fourth Marines advanced further south. Fortunately, the fixed Japanese shore defense guns at Tinian Town were trained seaward to repel the anticipated American landings there, and were useless to defend against the Marines' overland advance from the north.

On the Fourth Division left, adjacent to the Second Marine Division, the Twenty-Fifth Marines seized a Japanese airfield inland from Tinian Town without resistance. Most of the Twenty-Fifth Regiment's units then passed into Northern Landing Force or Fourth Division Reserve for the remainder of the Tinian campaign.

During the late afternoon of July 30, Ayresie's Twenty-Third Marines ended their reserve role, relieved the Twenty-Fifth Marines, and rejoined the southward advance with the Twenty-Fourth Marines to their right or west.

The Marines now approached the most formidable remaining terrain on Tinian. This obstacle consisted of a high, brushy plateau extending 5,000 yards from northeast to southwest and ending in steep cliffs just above the island's southeast coast. On this commanding ground, most of the surviving Japanese defense garrison now assembled to make their final stand. Opposite them, the Second Marine Division was poised to attack on the left or east, and the Twenty-Third and Twenty-Fourth Marines of the Fourth Marine Division were similarly positioned to attack on the right or west.

General Schmidt's operation order for July 31, 1944 called for an intense naval bombardment of Tinian's southeastern plateau by two battleships and three cruisers offshore, aided by Marine artillery. An extensive air bombardment then would occur, quickly followed by a ground attack. In the words of the Fifth Amphibious Corps commander, this attack would carry to Tinian's coastline and "annihilate the opposing Japanese."

The final defeat of the remaining Japanese troops on Tinian would be no easy task. On the left in the Second Division zone, steep cliffs rising to the plateau prevented a direct ascent. Near the center of the high land mass, access to the plateau was by a single, twisting dirt road exposed to Japanese observation and fire. To the west or far right, the slopes to the plateau were more manageable and could be climbed with relative ease.

On August 31, General Thomas Watson ordered the Second Marines of his Second Division to advance to the eastern base of the cliff, and block any attempts by Japanese to escape northward along Tinian's east coast. He then ordered the Sixth and Eighth Marines' assault units to fight their way up the winding road to the plateau's summit. Two platoons of

BLT 1/8 finally succeeded in reaching the top of the plateau in late afternoon and were followed by other units of BLT 2/8. These troops organized a tenuous but resilient defensive perimeter atop the plateau, aided by the late arrival of two thirty-seven millimeter anti-tank guns with their crews.

The Marines' positions were soon tested by a frenzied banzai attack, in which a force of some 600 Japanese assaulted the lines of 2/8. Defensive fires, including the devastating canister rounds of both late-joining thirty-seven millimeter guns, defeated the attacking Japanese. Substantial American casualties were incurred, but 200 Japanese, some of whom had approached within five yards of the Marine positions, lay dead. The surviving Japanese withdrew to the south.

In the Fourth Marine Division's area of responsibility to the west, the Twenty-Third Marines advanced with tanks in support to the base of the plateau after overcoming a well concealed and fortified forty-seven millimeter anti-tank gun emplacement. By nightfall, BLT 1/23, Ayresie's Company I, and Company L of 3/23, had climbed to the top of the plateau. With the late arrival of one company of 2/23, the Marines formed their perimeter defense. In the course of their advance up the plateau a 500 yard gap had opened between the Twenty-Third Marine units and the Second Division to the left. Patrols from I Company moved further eastward in an effort to link up with the Second Division, but contact could not be made.

Further to the right, the Twenty-Fourth Marines had attacked southward along Tinian's west coast, supported by

LVT(A)s keeping pace just offshore, until they reached a position near the southwestern base of the plateau.

On August 1, BLT 3/6 relieved 2/8, which had been hit hard by the previous night's banzai attack. BLT 1/8 had suffered fewer casualties, and it was soon joined by 3/8. These units advanced against moderate resistance and reached the edge of the plateau at the coast in their zone by noon.

In the zone of the Twenty-Third Marines, additional units reached the top of the plateau by midmorning on August 1. After adjusting their lines with those of I and L Companies and the single company from BLT 2/23, the combined units attacked against moderate but stubborn resistance to the edge of the plateau above the southeast coast, thus reaching the limit of their objective.

Below them, the three landing teams of the Twenty-Fourth Marines swept from west to east, finally clearing stubborn pockets of Japanese in coastal caves, and among boulders and thick growth near the shore. On the evening of August 1, 1944, V Corps Commander Schmidt declared Tinian secure.

Such declarations did not mean that all remaining enemy had died or surrendered, or that all fighting on Tinian had ended. Some Japanese held out for months and even years on this and other conquered islands in the Pacific. In the predawn hours of August 2 on Tinian, some 200 well-armed Japanese attacked the command post of BLT 3/6 to the east of the Twenty-Third Marines. Although most of the Japanese attackers died, their attack had taken the lives of 3/6's commanding officer, Lieutenant Colonel John Easley, and a number of his Marines. These sporadic attacks continued for days as isolated groups of a few, or occasionally dozens of Japanese eschewed surrender and mounted banzai attacks, inevitably resulting in their own deaths at the cost of more Marine lives.

As the battle for Tinian neared its end, increasing numbers of civilians emerged from caves and other hiding places in response to loudly amplified assurances of humane treatment, and approached the advancing Marines. Many of these groups and individuals were forced by Japanese troops hiding among them to join them in self-destruction, in repetition of the horrendous spectacles on Saipan's northern coast. However, many more civilians on Tinian either believed the Americans' announcements, or were able to avoid suicide forced upon them by Japanese troops. Over 8,400 civilians had been received at American refugee camps on Tinian by August 4, 1944, where they received food, water, and medical treatment.

On August 3, 1944, the men of I Company either joined work parties ordered to perform the despised task of burying enemy dead , or were assigned to mop up, eliminating bypassed pockets of Japanese in BLT 3/23's zone of action.

"Mopping up," used in previous chapters, is, like declaring an island "secured," a somewhat misleading phrase as applied to Marines fighting Japanese in the Pacific. Marines were and are trained to plan and execute attacks aggressively, thus keeping the enemy off-balance and denying them the opportunity to organize and strengthen their defenses. If a stubborn pocket of resistance was encountered in the Pacific campaign, the momentum of the attack was not interrupted. Instead, the pocket was contained and bypassed to be eliminated by other units, including those assigned a reserve role in the area, while the advance continued apace. This was mopping up, and it was an extremely difficult and dangerous task. Marines were required to cautiously approach caves or other protected positions from which gunfire could and often did erupt without warning. If no response to calls for surrender was heard, the Marines were required to kill any Japanese troops who remained hidden, and either fought to the death or committed suicide rather than suffer the shame of surrender.

In this manner, I Company occupied itself from August 3 to 7, when it finally moved to an assembly area. On August 8, 1944, Ayresie and his squad boarded the *SS Jean Lafitte* for a twelve day return voyage to Camp Maui.

As their transport sailed eastward from Tinian, it left in its wake a Pacific island that would become the principal base for heavy US Army Air Corps B-29 bombers conducting devastating fire bomb attacks on major Japanese cities. Tinian later launched both B-29 flights that quickly and decisively forced the Japanese to surrender, ending World War II.

Tinian had cost the Second and Fourth Marine Divisions a combined 317 killed and 1,550 wounded before the island was declared secure on August 1, 1944. These American casualties were sobering but were far less than the total suffered by both Marine divisions on Saipan. FMF Pacific Commander Holland Smith later described the Tinian invasion as the "perfect amphibious operation in the Pacific war."

CHAPTER 9

PELELIU: A HARBINGER OF HELL

By the early fall of 1944, Ayresie was promoted to sergeant, and awarded the Purple Heart for his shrapnel wounds on Saipan. I Company and other units gradually received replacements for most of their losses on Saipan and Tinian. Ayresie now led a full heavy machine gun section in training for another unspecified "future operation." Meanwhile, a fierce battle 4,500 miles to the west of Maui established an ominous precedent for the Marines of the Fourth Division as they continued to fight through the central Pacific toward Japan.

As General MacArthur's forces advanced northwest from New Guinea in fulfillment of his well-publicized promise to return to the Philippines, the General insisted that his eastern flank be protected. In MacArthur's view, this required elimination of a threat posed by a Japanese airbase located on the island of Peleliu in the Palaus.

Operation Stalemate II, the invasion and occupation of Peleliu, was scheduled to commence on September 15, 1944. As that date approached, continuous attacks by US carrier-borne aircraft had so severely weakened Japanese aviation capability in the area that Peleliu no longer posed a significant danger to MacArthur's invasion of Leyte. Admiral "Bull"

Halsey went so far as to recommend as late as September 13, 1944 that the invasion of Peleliu be cancelled altogether. However, Admiral Chester Nimitz and the Joint Chiefs of Staff ordered, consistent with if not obedient to MacArthur's wishes, that Operation Stalemate II proceed as planned.

By capturing the Marshall Islands and Saipan, Tinian, and Guam in the Marianas, Marines of the Second, Third, and Fourth Divisions, with certain US Army units fighting alongside, had breached Japan's outer ring of defenses in the central Pacific. The American advance now directly threatened Japan's "Zone of Absolute Defense," consisting of islands presenting the final obstacles to an attack on the Japanese home islands. The loss of these remaining bulwarks was considered intolerable. Japan therefore implemented a major change in its defensive tactics and strategy to confront the approaching Americans.

At Saipan, Tinian, and in earlier battles, Japanese strategy called for defeating the attacking Marines at the water's edge. The intended result, which fortunately for the Americans never occurred, was annihilation of the invaders and denial of a foothold on the objective. Failing to achieve this outcome, Japanese commanders previously had ordered large scale counterattacks, some as early as the first night ashore, against the Marine beachhead. With a single exception attributable at least in part to poor defensive preparations on Saipan, such banzai attacks were no match for concentrated American firepower and supporting arms. In every case, these attacks invariably failed to dislodge the determined Marines. Their consistent result had been destruction of a large portion of the enemy's strength and the hastening of Japan's loss of yet another island.

After the fall of Saipan and Tinian, Japan realized that it could never achieve outright victory in the Pacific, nor even hold onto previously conquered islands that now lay in the path of the American advance. Yet Emperor Hirohito and many senior officers continued to hope that Japan might force a negotiated end to World War II.

Japanese military commanders now resolved to alter their strategy and tactics by fighting a war of attrition, employing strong and elaborate defenses in depth. Future amphibious invasions still would be strongly opposed at the shoreline with infantry, mortars, and artillery. However, Japan's main defensive forces would no longer be ordered to fling themselves against well-defended American lines in frenzied banzai attacks. Troops defending islands in Japan's absolute zone of defense were now commanded to remain in place inside well-fortified and concealed positions, and to inflict maximum possible American casualties until they were killed. If alive and lacking the means to resist, Japanese soldiers were ordered to commit suicide. Japan's latest incarnation of the Code of Bushido, which had encouraged wasteful, self-defeating attacks often fueled by sake, now inspired its soldiers to slay as many attacking Marines as they could before dying a glorious death, if necessary, by their own hand. "Seven lives for the emperor," was the order issued by Colonel Kunio Nakagawa to his determined troops, echoing the words of the late General Saito.

Peleliu lent itself perfectly to this mission. The island's airfield, located on flat terrain near the chosen western landing beaches, was its main strategic asset, and Nakagawa's troops were as determined to hold it as the Marines were to take it. But the heart of Peleliu's defense lay in the rugged Umurbrogol highlands extending north from the airfield. This fractured, erratic series of steep coral and limestone peaks, ravines, and ridges was honeycombed by hundreds of connected natural and man-made caves, some with retractable steel doors guarding artillery positions, and others with features effectively sheltering the Japanese and their plentiful automatic weapons.

Against this teeming and near-impregnable fortress sheltering some 9,000 fanatic, well-trained, and motivated defenders, came the men of the First Marine Division. Their Division Commander, Major General William Rupertus, predicted that his Marines would secure the island in two or three days. The general even objected strongly to his superiors' insistence that a US Army regiment stand by as his reserve force. Rarely, if ever, has a commander's prediction of the human cost of his men's battle been so in error.

The September 15, 1944 landings were violently opposed, particularly from artillery and anti-boat guns in protected positions flanking the invasion beaches. Over 1,000 Marine casualties were suffered during the first two days. Following this ordeal, the First Marine Regiment swung northward and attacked into the teeth of the Umurbrogol's hidden and interlocking fields of artillery, mortar, and machine gun fire. Again and again, the Marines attacked frontally against the Japanese, who rained all manner of grazing and plunging fire upon them from their commanding positions. Day after day, as temperatures soared well above one hundred degrees and fresh water supplies were exhausted, Marines steadfastly attacked, and their losses alarmingly mounted. By the sixth day of the battle, the First Marines' overall casualties had exceeded 50 percent, with some units having lost in excess of 70 percent of their men.

Finally, the First Marines were pulled from the battle and relieved by the US Army's Eighty-First Infantry Regiment, over the persistent objections of their own regimental commander and those of General Rupertus. Both officers seemed almost oblivious to a degree of suffering and loss that threatened to eliminate the First Marine Regiment as a viable military unit.

These unsustainable losses did not result from the massed banzai attacks previously seen in Pacific invasions. The Japanese eventually lost Peleliu and their entire defending force virtually to a man. However, in the process they had, as instructed by their superiors in Tokyo, almost bled the First Marine Regiment and several other units white. They did so by remaining concealed in their protective defensive positions, and simply killing American Marines for as long as they and their abundant ammunition supplies held out.

This disciplined strategy, by which the Japanese sought to blunt American determination through sacrificing their own troops to Pyrrhic victories by Marines, would be employed in defense of every remaining Pacific objective, including Japan itself.

CHAPTER 10

IWO JIMA

Kitano Point

End of Day
8 March

5
3
Airfield No. 3

3
4
2 23

5
3
Airfield No. 2
Hill 382
3 24

3
4 "Amphitheater"
"Turkey Knob"

Tachiiwa Pt

East Boat Basin

Blue 2

Blue 1

Airfield No. 1
Yellow 2
Yellow 1
4th MarDiv

Red 2
Red 1
Mt. Suribachi
Green 1
5th MarDiv

Iwo Jima.

Aloha, Maui

As Christmas of 1944 approached, it was clear to Ayresie and his machine gunners that a large operation against another Pacific island was approaching. Hardly a week passed from early December, 1944 until mid-January of 1945 without a large scale embarkation and practice landing. On each exercise the Twenty-Third Marines attacked the shores of Maalea Bay or Kahoolawe Island in exactly the same manner. Multiple waves of the First and Second Battalions landed from left to right in the assault, with the Third Battalion following close behind. Their orders were the same: Assault "Yellow Beaches One and Two" of the unknown target, and attack inland to seize an enemy airfield.

Following another Hawaiian practice landing on January 17, 1945, transports bearing the Fourth Marine Division bypassed Maui's Kahului Harbor and steered directly toward Pearl Harbor. Word was passed that 25 percent of the troops would rotate to receive shore liberty in Honolulu. Ayresie and Ski, aboard the *USS Lowndes* with Battalion Landing Team 3/23, made plans for the first opportunity they would have to go ashore.

Tom Savery had survived his June 15, 1944 shrapnel wounds on Saipan, and thereafter experienced a harrowing evacuation. The high rate of D-Day casualties had slowed the flow of wounded from Saipan's Southwestern shore to ships capable of receiving and treating them. Tom's wounds were again dressed by a corpsman as Japanese mortars and artillery continued to pound Charan Kanoa. Finally, he was helped to the beach and carried on a stretcher aboard an LVT with other wounded Marines. This small, marginally seaworthy craft then churned through surf and swells toward ships anchored thousands of yards offshore.

As the LVT bearing Tom cautiously eased against the side of the nearest ship designated to receive wounded, a navy deck officer high above the pitching craft called out, "We're full," blithely waved it off, and gestured toward a vessel anchored in the distance. The Marine LVT driver obediently withdrew and gunned his LVT with its vulnerable human cargo toward the designated ship. There, yet another deck officer waved the craft away for the same reason. As ocean swells continued to mount and darkness gathered, a third ship's officer waved the LVT off. The angry and thoroughly frustrated LVT driver demanded that his wounded passengers be off-loaded and taken aboard then and there. The naval officer relented, and the LVT and deck crewmen worked quickly as each wounded Marine, including the thoroughly unnerved Tom, was hoisted high into the air, lowered to the vessel's main deck, and carried below.

Tom was transported to Oahu, where he began a course of treatment and rehabilitation at Aeia Heights Naval Hospital in the hills above Pearl Harbor. As he rested quietly there on January 25, 1945, the door of his room burst open, admitting the grinning Ayresie and Ski. The two friends last had seen Tom lying wounded and bleeding inside the wrecked structure in Charan Kanoa, as Ayresie led his squad, less Tom and the unfortunate Bob Avery, inland toward Mount Fina Susu.

Ayresie and Ski were happy to see their original number one gunner, who still faced weeks of treatment before he would be cleared for duty and rejoin I Company. Tom asked Ayresie how Ski and he had managed to get to Honolulu. Ayresie explained that, after the Division's last landing exercise on Maui, the *Lowndes* had sailed for Pearl Harbor. Aeia Heights was their first stop on shore liberty.

The visit with Tom was not lengthy because the Fourth Division was shipping out. As always, security dictated that the objective not yet be disclosed to troops. All Ayresie and Ski could tell Tom was that the operation was "something big," and that their practice landings indicated that 3/23 would be following the regiment's First and Second Battalions onto some island's Yellow Beaches to seize an enemy airfield.

Ski and Ayresie also had learned that Marines from at least one additional division, the recently formed Fifth, also were on shore liberty in Honolulu from ships in Pearl Harbor. They correctly assumed that the Fifth Division would be in on the same operation.

The Marines' target was Iwo Jima.

The Objective

Operation Forager had provided excellent bases in the Marianas on Saipan, Tinian, and Guam for General Curtis Lemay's B-29 superfortresses to launch long-range bombing attacks against strategic targets in Japan's home islands. Directly astride the heavy bombers' course to Tokyo and other Japanese cities lay the bleak, volcanic island of Iwo Jima, with two operational airfields, and one additional field under construction.

The 2,700 mile round trip missions from the Marianas to Japan were difficult and costly for Lemay's B-29s. In addition to frequent mechanical problems, the bombers were exposed to attack over their targets, and ran a double gauntlet of Japanese fighter planes based on Iwo Jima which intercepted them going and coming. Iwo Jima's radar also gave advance warning of the approaching bombers to fighters and anti-aircraft crews defending Japanese cities. Damaged B-29s unable to return to their bases in the Marianas were forced to ditch at sea, resulting in loss of the aircraft, and too often their crews. US strategists knew that Iwo Jima's existing airfields could be adapted quickly to accommodate emergency landings, repairs, and takeoffs by B-29s.

As a further strategic advantage, possession of Iwo Jima's airfields would enable American fighters based there to provide full-time escort for Marianas-based B-29s between the island and their Japanese targets.

Japanese leaders were well aware that this was the most militarily useful of their Nanpo Shoto Island chain extending southward from Tokyo Bay, and that its attack by the Americans was inevitable. They also knew that the island's loss would expose the nation's population and industrial targets to ever more frequent and devastating bombing attacks preceding a full scale American invasion. Finally, holding and defending this Japanese outpost, which was a component part of the Tokyo Prefecture, was a matter of honor to the Japanese.

For all of these reasons, Japan's military leadership would spare no effort to deny this small but critical part of their empire to the hated Americans. At the very least, the Japanese were determined to exact such a fearful toll for its loss that America would seek a negotiated peace that would preserve their divine emperor's rule, and perhaps enable them to retain some of their mandated or captured Pacific possessions. For this daunting and likely sacrificial task, Prime Minister Hideki Tojo chose a fifty-five-year-old, thirty-year veteran army officer whose courage and tactical genius eventually earned the respect of the Marines fighting on Iwo Jima.

Lieutenant General Tadamichi Kuribayashi had fought in Manchuria and China, and had served a three-year tour of duty in the United States in the late 1920s. He recently had commanded Emperor Hirohito's own Imperial Guard in Tokyo. A true samurai from a long family tradition of military service, Kuribayashi readily accepted his critical assignment. He also embraced what to him was its certain outcome, writing to his wife, "You must not expect my survival."

Arriving on Iwo Jima during the second week of June, 1944, Kuribayashi had just over eight months to convert the eight square mile island into the ultimate killing ground. Here, the samurai general would elevate the defensive strategy and tactics encountered by the First Marine Division at Peleliu to a peak of lethality. Under his leadership and direction, Iwo Jima would be transformed into the most invulnerable and deadly island objective that invaders have encountered before or since.

Kuribayashi's first task was to relieve and replace several senior officers under his command who were reluctant or unwilling to forego the futile banzai attacks of the past, stand fast with their troops in secure defensive positions, and fight there to the death. While this reorganization of a stubborn cadre of commanders was being accomplished, Kuribayashi also managed to temper a long standing and counterproductive rivalry between his army and naval commanders, and meld the rival military units on Iwo Jima into a more cooperative defense garrison.

Every Japanese defender embraced and swore to obey Kuribayashi's "courageous battle vows." These commands were posted in defensive positions throughout the island and discovered by the Marines after it fell:

> Above all, we shall dedicate ourselves and our entire strength to the defense of this island; We shall grasp bombs, charge enemy tanks, and destroy them; We shall infiltrate into the midst of the enemy and annihilate

them; With every salvo, we will without fail kill the enemy; Each man will make it his duty to kill ten of the enemy before dying; Until we are destroyed to the last man, we shall harass the enemy with guerilla tactics.

Iwo Jima's small Japanese civilian population was evacuated to the home islands. Small schools, shops, and homes in villages such as Motoyama and Minami were leveled, denying the Americans shelter and exposing them to Japanese observation and fields of fire.

Kuribayashi and his staff meticulously inspected Iwo Jima's terrain and planned its defensive positions in depth. The island viewed from above has frequently been described as resembling a pork chop, with its long axis oriented from southwest to northeast. Its narrow, southernmost point was formed by Mount Suribachi, the highest point on Iwo Jima. The extinct volcano's 550-foot height above sea level provided observation for miles to the northeast and a commanding view of the entire length of both possible landing beaches.

From this narrow point, the island fanned outward over rolling terrain for some two miles. One mile from Suribachi's base, the main Japanese airfield, Airfield Number One, was constructed on a raised table of land.

The island continued to broaden north of the eastern landing beaches and rose to form the rocky, domed Motoyama plateau. Here, several hundred yards north of the first airfield, Iwo Jima's second airfield, Number Two, was located.

Still further northward, the island reached its greatest width of two and one-half miles. This northern portion of the island contained its most formidable and easily defended terrain, consisting of every conceivable geological obstacle, including irregular hills, rocky outcroppings, ridges, cliffs, and ravines, all extending to Iwo Jima's northern and eastern coastlines.

General Kuribayashi realized that Iwo Jima's eastern and western beaches extending some two miles northward from the base of Mount Suribachi were the only feasible landing sites. He also correctly deduced that the eastern coast was the Americans' most likely choice. Here, wave action had formed steeply banked terraces of coarse, black granular volcanic ash. The Americans were unaware that these features would seriously impede the movement of their troops, tanks, and vehicles.

Mount Suribachi formed a critical element of the island's defense. The Japanese immediately set about extending, connecting, and fortifying its caves and tunnels and fashioning concealed and protected firing positions in its northern slopes and about its base.

Marines landing on the eastern beaches below Suribachi would be exposed to Japanese observation, and direct fire from large caliber guns. From the north, numerous rocket emplacements and literally hundreds of artillery and mortar positions, all well-screened from air observation and air and naval bombardment, were accurately trained on the beaches and inland areas. Their fires could be quickly called in from Mount Suribachi and other high ground to the north.

By D-Day, February 19, 1945, over 600 large caliber guns and mortars had precisely preregistered their fires, covering practically every square yard of Iwo Jima's landing beaches, as well as areas inland. Buried minefields were placed in likely avenues of approach.

Kuribayashi's troops could not hope to repel and defeat the Marines' advance solely with their artillery, rockets, and mortars. The Japanese commander therefore had designed and supervised the building of extensive, mutually supporting ground defenses in depth. Hundreds of buried positions ranging from one-man "spider holes" to elaborate reinforced bunkers and pillboxes were prepared, from which deadly machine gun and rifle fire could be brought to bear from multiple directions. Mining engineers sent from Japan augmented miles of existing caves and tunnels in Iwo Jima's porous limestone and volcanic rock on Mount Suribachi and throughout other areas in the hills, ravines, and ridges to the north. Connected caves and tunnels were later found as deep as five levels, some containing well-equipped medical facilities for surgical treatment of wounded.

By D-Day on Iwo Jima, at least eleven of some seventeen planned miles of underground caves and tunnels linked the widespread, concealed cave entrances and firing positions, all giving cover to Japanese gunners and riflemen. This system also enabled defenders to move about unobserved to reoccupy positions which previously had been silenced and left to the rear as Marines advanced beyond them. Marines often would be forced to attack and secure such positions over and over again.

All of these Japanese preparations continued feverishly and unobserved in any useful detail by American intelligence until D-Day on Iwo Jima. The Marines of the Third, Fourth, and Fifth Divisions would land against an island fortified and prepared to a level as yet unseen in the Pacific campaign.

Operation Detachment

Ayresie and Ski reboarded the *USS Lowndes* after their visit with Tom Savery, and on January 27, 1945, the attack transport weighed anchor and sailed westward from Pearl Harbor with its convoy. After nine days at sea, the *Lowndes* anchored at Eniwetok Atoll and remained there for three days as more ships of the invasion fleet gathered. The convoy then sailed to Saipan, where from topside, Ayresie and Ski could make out Blue Beach One where they had landed eight months before, and the town of Charan Kanoa where they had lost Bob Avery. Finally, the *Lowndes* departed Saipan among the assembled invasion fleet, now numbering some 800 ships carrying over 70,000 embarked Marines, and sailed the final three day leg of the voyage to Iwo Jima.

American aircraft had conducted attacks against Iwo Jima from the Marianas and carriers at sea intermittently for several months. During this period, naval and Marine commanders began to discuss the preparatory naval bombardment for the invasion.

Fleet Marine Force, Pacific Commander Holland M. Smith, and Fifth or "V" Amphibious Corps Commander General Harry Schmidt had the benefit of whatever intelligence studies were available long before D-Day of Operation Detachment. More importantly, their extensive experience in Pacific Island invasions dating from Tarawa and Roi-Namur had demonstrated the importance of extensive bombing and naval gunfire preparation preceding amphibious invasions against the Japanese. Accordingly, Generals Smith and Schmidt requested in late October, 1944 a preinvasion naval bombardment lasting ten days. Both strongly felt this length of preparation was needed to destroy a substantial amount of Japanese targets, and to reduce casualties to their Marines as much as possible.

This request would require approval by Admiral Kelly Turner, overall commander of the Pacific Fleet's amphibious forces. Against all logic and common sense in the view of Marines to this day, this critical issue directly affecting the fate of troops ashore was not to be decided by the most senior Marine commanders in the Pacific theater. Instead, the nature and length of preparatory fires ultimately were to be decided by senior naval officers, whose primary functions were to select strategic objectives, carry Marines safely to those objectives, and land them. Thereafter, US Navy commanders remained at sea in their ships, delivering supplies, receiving and treating casualties, and providing naval gunfire and air support on call while the Marines ashore fought the Japanese.

To the dismay of Generals Smith and Schmidt, Admiral Turner reduced the naval gunfire support for Operation Detachment to three days.

There then commenced a series of exchanges more appropriate to vendors and buyers haggling in a marketplace than to American service branches cooperating to win a war. General Schmidt submitted another proposal, supported by a thorough staff study, for nine days of preparatory bombardment. Turner refused this request as well, stating that three days of naval gunfire would be adequate, considering "limitation of ships, ammunition, and time."

General Schmidt, almost in desperation, approached the admiral and asked for a single additional day—a total of four days of preinvasion naval gunfire and air bombardment. This final request was strongly endorsed by General Holland Smith, who unequivocally predicted that fewer days of preparatory fires would contribute to casualties in excess of any yet seen in the Pacific. Admiral Turner initially seemed convinced that he should grant this request for an additional day of preparatory fires so fervently made and supported by the two most senior Marine officers in the Pacific theater. However, after consulting with subordinate commanders, he again refused even one additional day of naval gunfire. Finally, on January 2, 1945, General Holland Smith repeated his own request for a single additional day of naval gunfire and was again refused.

The general's understandable frustration and bitterness toward the navy, shared by many Marines, persisted as long as he lived as reflected in his personal memoir, *Coral and Brass*: "Thus we were defeated—a group of trained and experienced land fighters, our full realization of the necessity for naval gunfire based on many previous island operations—again overridden by the naval mind."

Dog Day

After three days of preparatory fire and aerial bombardments, February 19, 1945 dawned clear and calm, with sea conditions described as "perfect for landing."

In this largest Pacific Island invasion to date, the newly formed Fifth Marine Division would land on three eastern beaches, extending from Suribachi's base some 1,500 yards to the north, designated Green One, Red One, and Red Two. The Fourth Marine Division's assault units would land on three adjacent beaches to the north, Yellow One, Yellow Two, and Blue One. Blue Beach Two, to the immediate north of Blue One, lay just under steep cliffs with concealed positions sheltering large caliber Japanese direct fire weapons. For this reason, Blue Beach Two was deemed untenable for landing, and would be occupied once the commanding cliffs were secured by Marines landing on Blue One.

Operation Detachment's plan called for the Fifth Division's Twenty-Eighth Marines to attack rapidly across the island's narrow neck just north of Mount Suribachi, and then flank to the left and capture the mountain itself. The Twenty-Seventh Marines would land just to the north, advance across the island's isthmus, and attack northward along the western coast to an ambitiously designated 0-1 line.

BLTs 1/23 and 2/23 of the Fourth Division's Twenty-Third Marines were assigned to lead the assault on Yellow Beaches One and Two, as practiced repeatedly in Hawaii and laboriously reviewed over maps and rubber contoured models of Iwo Jima en route. These units would then advance inland to seize Airfield One. Ayresie's BLT 3/23 would remain on call aboard the *Lowndes* as regimental reserve. The Twenty-Fifth Marines, after landing and seizing Blue Beach One, would proceed inland and pivot northward to seize the cliffs and high ground overlooking Blue Beach Two.

The Third Marine Division would remain offshore on call as the V Amphibious Corps floating reserve.

The original operation plan provided for the Fifth Marine Division on the left and Fourth Marine Division on the right to attack northward on the second day, capturing both airfields and securing the entire island in at little as three and no more than five days. This schedule would not be met.

The men of the assault waves of the Fourth and Fifth Divisions awoke early and nervously downed their breakfast

156

of steak and eggs on the mess decks of their LSTs. Armed to the teeth, the assault troops boarded their LVTs and launched from LSTs before dawn. At 0830, the leading assault waves, followed by other waves three minutes apart, crossed the line of departure and churned shoreward. The first wave of LVTs hit the invasion beaches at 0903.

Hurrying from their LVTs, the Marines immediately sank to and above the tops of their boondockers into loose, black volcanic ash and residue, the storied "black sand" of Iwo Jima. This surface was extremely difficult to negotiate and virtually impassable to wheeled and many tracked vehicles. The Marines struggled to climb the steep, loose terraces of ash and clear the beaches for succeeding waves.

The Japanese did not immediately bring significant anti-boat or other fires to bear against the early assault waves. As Marines in those waves came ashore and began to move inland, Japanese guns still remained oddly silent, except for occasional mortar rounds and scattered small-arms fire.

Almost an hour later, more assault waves had landed in sequence, and thousands of Marines had moved inland as much as 500 yards in some sectors. As these Marines continued to come ashore and move inland, they became an increasingly target-rich environment—a carpet of Marines and their supporting weapons, equipment, and supplies almost two miles long and hundreds of yards deep, with LVTs, bogged-down vehicles, and equipment and supplies about the area. At that moment, Kuribayashi unleashed a hellish storm of his preregistered artillery, mortar, and rocket fire from Suribachi and positions to the north, while Japanese gunners in blockhouses, concealed pillboxes, and spider holes commenced accurate, grazing machine gun and rifle fire.

Suddenly, Marines throughout the beachhead were receiving intense and accurate fire from their flanks, from ahead, and from the sky above, while the loose, black sand impeded their movements and made digging in for shelter almost impossible. One surviving Marine described his efforts to dig in as "like digging in a bin of wheat."

As Marines attempted to spot the sources of enemy fire and struggled for limited cover, M4 Sherman tanks aboard LCMs were called in to support the advance. These tanks, and several armored LVTs seeking to clear the beach, were challenged by deteriorating surf conditions and exploding mines buried in areas where likely beach exits existed.

Through this heaviest and most accurate concentration of Japanese artillery, mortar, and rocket fire that Marines had yet faced in the Pacific, the Fifth Division struggled across the island's narrow isthmus at the foot of Mount Suribachi, while the assault teams of the Twenty-Fourth and Twenty-Fifth Marines, steadily taking casualties with almost every yard gained, fought toward Airfield Number One.

Ayresie Ashore

The *Lowndes* had arrived in the transport area off Iwo Jima shortly after 0600 on D-Day. Companies I and L were prepared to land when ordered on one of the Yellow Beaches as the first of six waves of BLT 3/23. At 0640, Ayresie's machine gun section "davit loaded" at deck level aboard their LCVPs which were then lowered into the sea. By sunrise, all assault waves of BLT 3/23 were circling seaward of the line of departure awaiting the order to land.

Despite the fierce struggle ashore, that order was long in coming. The initial anticipation and excitement of the Marines aboard their circling craft resolved to impatience. After circling in their LCVPs for over five hours, BLT 3/23 received the regimental commander's order to land on Yellow Beach One. Seventeen minutes later, Ayresie's assault wave hit Yellow Beach One and immediately came under the fusillade of artillery, mortar, and rocket fire that had rained down for hours on the earlier assault waves.

I and L Companies struggled through the coarse black ash of Yellow Beach One, passing the bleeding, dismembered, and often unrecognizable bodies of Marine dead. Kuribayashi's preplanned heavy weapons fires had taken their toll, and were continuing to do so. In the words of *Time* magazine combat correspondent Robert Sherrod, the Marines landing on Iwo Jima "died with the greatest possible violence."

BLT 3/23's orders were to attack toward the first airfield and relieve the badly mauled First Battalion. Suffering casualties practically every minute, Companies I and L continued to push forward.

Shortly after I Company had landed, Ayresie's popular Second Platoon commander, First Lieutenant Howard "Smiley" Johnson, paused briefly to ask young Private First Class Walter Berry of Belleville, Illinois how he was doing. Berry responded to Lieutenant Johnson that he was doing OK. Just as the lieutenant acknowledged Berry's response and moved on to organize his platoon, he was killed with three other Marines by an exploding Japanese mortar round. The unit's platoon sergeant immediately took command of the Second Platoon, and Companies I and L finally reached the eastern edge of the main runway of Airfield One. By 1700, BLT 3/23 had relieved the embattled Marines of 1/23.

The Fourth Marine Division's assault waves suffered heavy casualties in their advance to Airfield One. While preregistered artillery, mortar, and rocket fire pounded their ranks from Mount Suribachi's base and slopes and from concealed positions to the north, accurate machine gun and rifle fire punished the attacking Marines from their front, flanks, and even from unseen and bypassed positions to their rear.

As daylight waned, Ayresie placed his machine gun squads in the most defensible positions near the raised runway of Airfield One. Their first night on Iwo Jima gave no respite to the Marines. Although the Japanese did not counterattack in force, infiltrators, some of whom crawled through buried drains under Airfield One's eastern runway, approached their lines in darkness. Other Japanese lobbed or rolled grenades onto their defensive positions, while artillery and mortar fire continued to fall on the beaches and inland throughout the night. The riflemen and machine gunners of I and L Companies engaged these Japanese infiltrators, and the night passed without further Marine advances or loss of ground to the enemy.

The first day of their battle for Iwo Jima had cost the Fourth and Fifth Marine Divisions some 1,800 casualties, over 500 of whom were killed or later died of their wounds. On the landing beaches where Japanese rounds continued to fall, some wounded Marines who lay waiting for evacuation suffered further wounds or were killed.

The Fourth and Fifth Divisions had been forced to halt well short of their theoretical and unrealistic 0-1 line, which would have represented capture of Mount Suribachi by the Fifth Division, the Fourth Division's capture of Airfield One and a portion of Airfield Two, and capture by the V Amphibious Corps of approximately one-third of the entire island. However, the two Marine divisions had landed over 30,000 troops and had established a substantial beachhead. The United States Marines were on Iwo Jima to stay.

At 0830 on February 20, D plus one, Companies I and L with the support of Sherman tanks continued to lead 3/23's assault, pivoting clockwise to the northeast to seize all of

Airfield One. The going was slow and costly under heavy artillery, mortar, and small arms fire, but Airfield One was taken. Companies I and L dug in just to its northeast, at the limit of their advance.

On the morning of February 21, D plus two, Company I, and Company K, which had passed through and relieved Company L, continued the attack northeastward in an effort to capture Airfield Two on the Motoyama Plateau. Here, concealed Japanese dual-purpose guns sighted along Airfield Two's runways had clear views of the attacking Marines and unleashed deadly direct fire at them. Japanese artillery and mortars also continued to fire from unseen positions to the north, while rifle and machine guns from block houses, pillboxes, and concealed spider holes spat fire on any visible Marines. By the early afternoon of D plus two, this attack had gained at most 150 yards. As Sherman tanks attempted to lead the advances, Marines accompanied them in support. In these conditions, the powerful tanks often were an invitation for the Japanese to bombard the nearby Marines with mortars and artillery.

American efforts to bring naval gunfire and Marine artillery to bear in this area generally failed. As soon as the first American volleys struck, Japanese gunners withdrew into their sheltering caves and passageways, many with offset entrances, waited until American fires lifted, and then quickly returned to their firing positions.

3/23 finally was forced to halt in late afternoon. By this time, Company I, which had borne the brunt of the attack to seize Airfield One, had been "pinched out" in the advance, was relieved by Company K, and withdrew several hundred yards to the rear to reorganize.

Near midnight of D plus two, a night attack by some 200 Japanese moved against the lines of 3/23's K and L Companies. These attacking Japanese were in the open, a rare occasion on Iwo Jima. Their attempt was defeated by Marine artillery and the disciplined fire of riflemen and machine gunners. This attack finally deteriorated into isolated infiltration attempts that were also repulsed, their only accomplishment to deprive the weary Marines of much-needed sleep.

On Iwo Jima and elsewhere in the Pacific, the Japanese owned the night. Infiltration by these masters of stealth was expressly ordered by the third of General Kuribayashi's six battle vows, and was both a nuisance and a constant threat. For this reason, among others, the Marines largely conceded the night to the enemy. At the end of each day's advance, Marines made certain that adjacent units were strongly linked with each other on the most favorable ground, and prepared their own protected and mutually supporting defensive positions. Critical components of these defenses were the Browning heavy machine guns and their crews.

From their defensive positions, Marines under standard operating procedure could be ordered to fire without hesitation on any person moving above ground to their front or flanks. This was particularly true if a Marine's verbal challenge did not receive the proper, designated response.

These passwords and their countersigns were selected to frustrate Japanese efforts to pronounce them. If the challenge received the reply "rorripop" instead of a designated "lollipop," Marines confidently blazed away.

By the morning of D plus three, February 22, 1945, the Twenty-Third Marine Regiment's combined casualties from three days of continuous fighting against strong Japanese resistance and concentrated automatic and heavy weapons fire mandated reinforcement and replacements. On the afternoon of D plus two, one regiment of the Third Marine Division, the Twenty-First Marines, had landed and was ordered to relieve the Twenty-Third Marines. By 1130 on February 22, the Twenty-First Marines had replaced the Twenty-Third in their zone of action, and the Twenty-Third Marines, now in V Corps Reserve, relocated southward to positions in the vicinity of Airfield One. Although the airfield was now in American hands, no area of Iwo Jima, front or rear, was immune from harassing artillery, mortar, and sniper fire.

The three battalion combat teams of the Twenty-Third Marines remained in this assembly area throughout the day and night. Sporadic artillery and mortar fire continued to fall in this "rear" area, causing occasional casualties and again serving to rob the weary Marines of rest.

Early on D plus four, February 23, 1945, Ayresie's battalion was ordered to another assembly area still further to the southwest, and at 1330, 3/23 occupied an area well less than a mile from the base of Mount Suribachi. From this area,

Ayresie and other I Company Marines could observe the second and larger American flag, which had replaced a smaller flag first raised on Suribachi's peak earlier that day.

Many Marines approached and even climbed Mount Suribachi that day. Ayresie would have had no difficulty reaching Suribachi on foot, either alone or in the company of others. By this time, Ayresie knew that I Company and his machine gun section would be moving northward to continue the attack on Iwo Jima's defenses. With BLT 3/23 in its reserve role, he had both time and opportunity to etch a message on his canteen.

On the morning of D plus five, February 24, I Company received seventy replacements. The Second Platoon, to which Ayresie's machine gun squads were attached, received a new platoon commander, Lieutenant Harcourt "Hawk" Waller, a tall, handsome native of Augusta, Georgia. Waller had grown impatient with Princeton University's ROTC program and had enlisted in the Marine Corps. Following his boot training at Parris Island, Hawk completed officer training at Quantico, Virginia, and was commissioned a second lieutenant upon his graduation from Princeton in late May of 1943.

After reporting to the Marine detachment at Ford Island, Pearl Harbor, and performing garrison duties as a guard and legal officer, Lieutenant Waller put in for a combat assignment. His request was granted. Within days, he received orders to Camp Maui and joined a replacement draft bound for Iwo Jima.

*Lieutenant Harcourt Waller in downtown Honolulu
before departing for Camp Maui and Iwo Jima.*

By the time he took command of I Company's Second
Platoon on Iwo Jima, Lieutenant Waller knew that he was
replacing a popular, experienced, and highly respected officer in Smiley Johnson. Fortunately, Waller had the good sense
in this, his first combat assignment, to respect, observe, and
learn from his more experienced noncommissioned officers

and enlisted men. Many of these Marines, including Ayresie and Ski, had fought and defeated the Japanese at Roi-Namur, Saipan, and Tinian. Watching, listening, and learning, Hawk soon earned the respect of the platoon for his intelligence, his personal courage, and his decisiveness under fire.

Among Hawk Waller's most trusted and experienced mentors and comrades in arms was Ayresie. Hawk wrote approvingly of Ayresie, calling him his "machine gun sergeant," whom he gave a "free hand with his guns." The two men would fight closely together in the heat of I Company's battles to come.

On the afternoon of February 24, D plus five, after receiving replacements and reorganizing, I Company again moved northeastward with the Twenty-Third Marines and assembled in an area just south of Airfield Two. There, 3/23 received orders to move forward on the following morning to pass through and relieve the Twenty-Fourth Marines. The Third Battalion would again lead the Twenty-Third Marines' assault to the northeast.

At dusk on D plus five, I Company formed a defensive position near the line of departure for the following day's attack. As darkness fell, Lieutenant Waller found that the field telephone lines from his Second Platoon Command Post or "CP" to that of I Company, and to the First Platoon one hundred yards to the rear, had been cut by Japanese infiltrators. Just before dawn the sounds of rapid rifle fire arose from the First Platoon's area, and Japanese were seen creeping stealthily toward the Second Platoon's positions from the rear. Ayresie's machine guns and the riflemen of the Second Platoon opened fire, killing most of the advancing Japanese. However, one determined Japanese soldier continued toward Waller. The lieutenant raised his carbine to meet the attack, but several of his men were too close to his line of fire. He called out quickly to his young runner, who dispatched the infiltrator with his M1 rifle.

In frenzied violation of General Kuribayashi's battle vows, cries of "banzai, banzai" now erupted from the attacking Japanese to the Second Platoon's rear. The First Platoon was under heavy attack by forty to fifty Japanese who had attacked from unsealed caves or tunnels to the Marines' rear—a frequently encountered Japanese tactic. Many of the Japanese wielded samurai swords, and three Japanese so armed reached the First Platoon's command post. The First Platoon commander killed two attackers with his carbine, but the third swung his sword and severed the young lieutenant's hand at the wrist with a single stroke. The determined officer killed the swordsman by firing shots from the .45 caliber pistol grasped in his remaining hand.

Dawn found I Company's First Platoon decimated. Its platoon commander's wound eventually required amputation of his entire arm. Eight members of the platoon were killed in the attack, some by sword wounds; over twenty men were wounded and out of action.

At 0930 on D plus six, February 25, Companies K and L of 3/23 attacked eastward from their line of departure toward an area of high ground called "Charlie Dog Ridge," as Company I followed in trace in reserve. Other units to their right advanced in a parallel direction. Resistance was heavy along 3/23's front; Companies K and L were met by heavy machine gun and rifle fire from their flanks and ahead, and received mortar fire from more distant Japanese positions. Gains were minimal and substantial casualties were suffered, but by the end of the day, the three companies of 3/23 held all of Airfield Two, and were tied into defensive positions some 250 yards to the west of their next day's objective.

The Hardest Ground

At the end of the first week's fighting on Iwo Jima, elements of three Marine divisions stood shoulder to shoulder, prepared to attack to the northeast into the teeth of the main Japanese "cross-island" defenses. Their mission: to destroy the Japanese defenders in their assigned sectors, and secure the island as a vital base supporting American heavy B-29s attacking the Japanese home islands, and their fighter escorts.

On the left, the Fifth Marine Division, having captured Mount Suribachi and its surrounding ground, would attack northward to Kitano Point in a zone bordered on the west by Iwo Jima's west coast. In the center, two regiments of the Third Marine Division would attack across the Motoyama Plateau to the northern end of the island. On the right, the Fourth Division's zone of action would be bounded on the left by the Third Division and on the right by Iwo Jima's east coast. Shifting battle conditions in each division's zone would dictate adjustments, but this general plan of attack would hold.

The sector of Iwo Jima assigned to the Fourth Marine Division, which lay generally to the east of Airfield Two, is widely considered to have held the most difficult and forbidding terrain on the island. The area rivaled, if not exceeded Peleliu's Umurbrogal in defensibility and unapproachability, and consisted of a maze of rocky hills, abrupt upthrusts of volcanic stone and coral, cliffs, and steep ridges cut by ravines meandering toward the eastern shore and Tachiiwa Point.

General Kuribayashi assumed that Iwo Jima would eventually fall, and obviously understood this particular area's tactical potential for inflicting maximum Marine casualties. His commanders had placed hundreds of hidden and fortified artillery and mortar positions, pillboxes, and even several partially buried Japanese tanks in this area. Throughout the zone, concealed Japanese machine gunners and snipers had interlocking and mutually supporting fields of fire covering every direction from which Marines could approach. Further to the northeast of these defensive positions, concealed rocket launchers, artillery pieces, and mortars could bring their fires to bear practically anywhere within the zone.

The principal, but not the only deadly feature of this area was "Hill 382" located some 250 yards to the northeast of the end of Airfield Number Two's east-west runway. Hill

382, named like other military terrain features for its height in feet above sea level, was the highest point on northern Iwo Jima. A bombed-out radar screen at its summit caused some Marines to refer to it as "radar hill." Its irregular heights afforded a commanding view to the south and east.

As yet unknown to the Twenty-Third Marines, Hill 382 was a major focal point of Kuribayashi's cross island defenses. Its numerous caves and tunnels held multiple concealed apertures for Japanese heavy weapons and machine guns. Deep, multi-level tunnels and caves made sheltered Japanese gunners invulnerable to American artillery, naval gunfire, and air attacks. As Marines closely approached these defenders, American artillery could no longer provide support. Hill 382 could only be taken by infantry and combat engineers closing with their rifles, flame throwers, grenades, and powerful explosives. Sherman tanks, normally a strong and effective aid to advancing Marines, would find it extremely difficult to negotiate the area's rough terrain.

One half mile to Hill 382's south near the end of a looping, irregular ridge lay an ugly, unnatural looking rocky pinnacle. Near its top was a concrete blockhouse with steel-reinforced concrete walls several feet thick. This pinnacle and its base were honeycombed with reinforced and well-camouflaged firing positions, all designed to provide mutual support. Marines locating and attacking a position in or near the pinnacle would be exposed to fire from other unseen positions nearby. This companion to Hill 382 came to be called "Turkey Knob."

To the west of Turkey Knob lay a relatively flat, natural bowl, resembling, and therefore called the "Amphitheater." This area was surrounded in part by ridges honeycombed with the usual connected and concealed caves and tunnels, with firing positions reinforced by stone and concrete. These concealed caves and tunnels sheltered Japanese heavy weapons and skilled machine gunners and snipers.

Together, Hill 382, Turkey Knob, and the Amphitheater formed a triad of fortified, mutually supporting defensive positions that were designed and intended to reap a fearsome toll on any attacking Marines. The area encompassing these positions soon earned a grim but accurate nickname.

The Marines dubbed it the "Meat Grinder."

Hill 382

At 0730 on D plus seven, February 26, following an artillery preparation, Hawk Waller's Second Platoon of I Company led 3/23's attack directly against Hill 382, with the Third Platoon of I Company to its right and the Second Platoon of C Company, 1/23 to its left. Lieutenant Waller led two rifle squads in the assault, with his third squad and Ayresie's machine gun section following closely several yards behind.

For the first 150 yards, Waller and his advancing rifle squads met no enemy resistance. As they approached within one hundred yards of the hill, I Company's Third Platoon to the right was taken under fire by machine guns firing from concealed positions. Waller and his riflemen, now joined by Ayresie and his two machine gun squads, sprinted forward and quickly reached Hill 382. The Marines rushed up Hill 382's broken slopes and all reached the area comprising its crest without suffering casualties. Waller actually reached upward and touched a portion of the hill's wrecked radar antenna with his bare hand. To his Second Platoon's left, C Company's Second Platoon also gained the slopes. The Marines had taken Hill 382! Then, as the lieutenant later wrote, "all hell broke loose."

Hill 382 viewed from the west after it was secured. The remnants of the radar antenna are visible at its forward crest and scattered below.

Crouching among the rocks and crevices on the rough crest of Hill 382, the Marines were suddenly receiving heavy mortar and machine gun fire from high ground to their front and from both flanks. Although reasonably well sheltered, Waller and his men were pinned down. The cunning Japanese had allowed the assault platoons to reach and occupy Hill 382, only to be isolated and immobilized by heavy and accurate machine gun and mortar fire. The concealed Japanese guns also could easily slaughter reinforcements that might attempt to reach the objective.

Hawk Waller observed the protected positions of his two assault rifle squads and found that Ayresie also had made it to Hill 382 with two of his machine gun crews. The young lieutenant was learning fast in the heat of combat. He wisely allowed his experienced machine gun section leader discretion to assign his squads as best suited the situation. Ayresie realized that the platoon's limited cover on Hill 382 could not accommodate both machine guns, and relocated one of his crews to another position from which it could support the Third Platoon of I Company by fire.

Waller's only choice was to instruct his squad leaders to keep their men under cover from the heavy and accurate Japanese fire striking their position.

After several minutes, the lieutenant peered to the front from behind a large stone and observed a Japanese machine gun emplacement firing on I Company's Third Platoon to the right. Rising carefully and exposing as little of himself as he could, Waller fired several rounds from his carbine at the position. Within seconds, a machine gun burst slammed into the stone, missing his head by inches.

Carefully using all protection the terrain afforded, Waller now moved to check his men and asked if any had located sources of the incoming fire. None had. As he moved among the sheltering rocks on and near the crest of the hill, two Marines some distance away waved him back, and yelled that he was about to enter the field of fire of another concealed Japanese machine gun. As one of the Marines raised his arm to point toward the hidden Japanese gun position, he was struck squarely in the head by a burst of machine gun fire from yet another position and killed instantly. Although Waller already had experienced his baptism of fire and certainly had seen the bodies of Marines killed in action, this was his first experience observing the death of an I Company Marine before his own eyes. It would not be his last.

Contacting the Second Platoon of C Company, 1/23 on his left flank, Waller found that its platoon commander had suffered a serious leg wound but was commanding his men as well as he could from a covered position. This platoon had suffered a number of casualties, and appeared to be pinned down by the same machine gun that had killed the Marine attempting to point out its position to Waller.

The lieutenant now decided to locate and determine the state of Ayresie's second machine gun squad and the Third Platoon to his right. By this time, Waller had adopted a means of moving by pausing for an unpredictable interval behind cover and then bolting from cover to sprint at full speed to the next covered position. Shots rang out almost each time he moved, but his quickness, his luck, or rare instances of poor Japanese marksmanship spared him.

In this manner Waller reached the Third Platoon of I Company, now pinned down and led by its platoon sergeant. There, he learned that the Third Platoon commander and his runner had succeeded in locating a position from which machine gun fire had pinned them down. These two Marines bravely launched their own attack, periodically throwing hand grenades to cover their approach. As they gathered themselves and made a final rush forward to close with the machine gun position, both fell victim to the Japanese system of mutually supporting positions. Another hidden machine gun suddenly opened fire from their flank, killing them both. Hearing this, Waller instructed the platoon sergeant who had assumed command of the Third Platoon to sit tight and remain protected for the moment. He then returned by his intermittent "stop, wait, and dash" method to his command.

Waller now resolved to locate and destroy the machine gun position that continued to hold the flanking platoons at bay, and that had killed the Marine who had died trying to signal its location to him.

Recalling the general direction pointed out by this Marine, the lieutenant slowly worked himself to a better position from which he could observe the area. Peering again over a large boulder, he saw two figures in Marine dungarees standing in a shallow depression. The lieutenant rose carefully and waved them down. The two men stared back at him for a moment in surprise, and then quickly crouched down as a burst of Japanese machine gun fire struck the boulder behind which Waller had hidden. The men were Japanese soldiers wearing Marine Corps utilities they had stripped from Marine dead—a ploy often used by the Japanese in their efforts to approach unwary American troops.

At considerable risk, Waller had determined the precise location of the Japanese machine gun. Returning to his platoon, he retrieved a Browning Automatic Rifle, called a "BAR," and began to look about for an available M1 Garand rifle equipped with a grenade launcher. Ayresie quickly volunteered to join the lieutenant, and armed himself with an M1 rifle and grenade launcher. The two Marines, platoon commander and machine gun section leader, returned together to the point from which Waller had located the Japanese machine gun position and commenced a personal duel with its gun crew. As one, Waller and Ayresie silently rose on signal, raised their weapons, fired, and ducked. Ayresie's rifle grenade fell short, and Waller's BAR jammed. The exploding rifle grenade brought renewed volleys of Japanese machine gun fire at their position.

Lieutenant Waller and Ayresie returned to their original position and carefully retraced their steps forward to their protected vantage point, Waller now armed with his carbine, and Ayresie with the same M1 rifle and grenade launcher. A third Marine accompanied them with a BAR. Unfortunately, the powerful weapon carried by this Marine also jammed after firing a single round. Waller's carbine also misfired, and the three Marines were forced to drop to cover as the Japanese machine gun resumed firing before Ayresie could launch another rifle grenade.

Waller and Ayresie returned once more to engage the Japanese machine gun position, but their efforts were again frustrated, Waller's BAR fouled by Iwo Jima's volcanic ash and dust, and Ayresie's rifle and grenade simply lacking the range and accuracy to effectively engage the protected machine gun emplacement.

As the Marines returned again to their original position, intense Japanese mortar fire began to fall among them. Lieutenant Waller was temporarily knocked unconscious by an exploding round and received a flesh wound on his face. The BAR man was wounded by a shot in the stomach. Another Marine nearby was hit by machine gun fire.

Night was now approaching, and Hawk Waller was the only surviving and fully functioning officer among the three platoons that had initiated the day's attack on Hill 382. These units had occupied the objective but had suffered the loss through death or wounds of half their combined strength. In fact, I Company's Second and Third platoons had suffered as many casualties, killed and wounded, in their initial assault of Hill 382 as the number of replacements they had received three days before.

It was clear that the capture and securing of Hill 382 would require more artillery preparation, more fire support, and more troops in tenable positions than remained alive and uninjured on this objective. Lieutenant Waller now received radioed orders to withdraw the remaining Marines on and around Hill 382 to the rear to more favorable positions for the night.

This uncomplicated order from higher headquarters behind the front lines presented a difficult task for Lieutenant Waller and the three embattled platoons on and around Hill 382. Although most of these remaining Marines were in defilade and screened from the front by the ridge partially encompassing Hill 382, they were exposed to heavy, interlocking machine gun fire from both flanks covering the original approaches over which they were ordered to withdraw.

Lieutenant Waller again traversed the area to speak with the noncommissioned officers in charge of each of the other committed platoons and planned an orderly withdrawal. Ambulatory wounded Marines in each platoon moved carefully in pairs to the rear along a narrow route affording the best degree of protection from observant Japanese. The more seriously wounded were moved on ponchos carried by uninjured Marines.

Japanese gunners eagerly fired on corpsmen, stretcher bearers, and others attempting to treat or evacuate wounded men. To meet this threat, Lieutenant Waller used the remaining working radio on Hill 382 to call in a smoke screen masking the movements of the withdrawing troops.

The careful and well-organized withdrawal from Hill 382 over the fire-swept area was accomplished with the loss of one Marine killed and two wounded. This level of casualties was considered a positive in the deadly calculus of losses on Iwo Jima.

Depleted in the first of many assaults that would occur on Hill 382, I Company assembled in an area several hundred yards to the rear to regroup, resupply, and get whatever rest could be managed under the intermittent harassing Japanese fire. The company now numbered barely one hundred combat effective Marines. New replacements joined the unit the following morning.

At this point in the operation, rear echelon cooks, clerks, other Marines assigned to support duties, and additional inexperienced Marines in replacement drafts increasingly began to replace combat veterans killed or wounded in fierce fighting on and after February 19. Even with these inexperienced replacements, I Company, following two days in reserve with 3/23, could muster only two understrength rifle platoons, Ayresie's supporting machine gun crews, and the crews for two sixty millimeter mortars.

The steady attrition in Marine units dictated further changes. As combat efficiency reached and fell below 50

percent, division commanders began to attach rifle companies or battalion landing teams to larger units assigned to
a particular operation. Thus, on D plus ten, February 29,
3/23's I and K Companies were attached to the Twenty-Fifth
Marines' First Battalion, and Company L was attached to
2/25. For all practical purposes, I Company now became a
component infantry company of 1/25.

In these situations, Marine leadership and discipline
largely eliminated the confusion and disorganization that
might be expected in a similar melding of organizations.
Companies I and K were simply "loaned" to the commanding
officer of 1/25, who led these attached companies and their
officers, NCOs, and men as if they had served in his battalion since the February 1, 1944 invasion of Roi-Namur in the
Marshall Islands.

Turkey Knob

On the morning of March 2, D plus eleven, I Company
waited at its line of departure near the southern end of the
irregular, cave-riddled ridge extending southward from Hill
382 to Turkey Knob. Accurate Japanese fire had spat inces-
santly from fortified positions in the ridge, Turkey Knob,
and from the impervious blockhouse near its peak since the
Fourth Division had first entered the Meat Grinder.

*Turkey Knob viewed from the west, with the reinforced Japanese
blockhouse visible just over the crest of the low ridge.*

Before dawn, I Company and its two platoon leaders had
received their orders for the day's attack from 1/25's commanding officer. Waller's Second Platoon was to attack southward along the edge of the ridge toward Turkey Knob with two
Sherman tanks in support, while 1/25's Company B attacked
from the south. The two units were to converge simultaneously
on Turkey Knob, and jointly envelop and reduce this strong
point in a coordinated "pincer" movement.

At daybreak, Waller's Second Platoon and Ayresie's
machine gun section moved forward behind I Company's
Third Platoon. At a position 200 yards to the north of Turkey

Knob, the Third Platoon and Ayresie's machine gun section halted and took up positions to support the attack on Turkey Knob. Waller's Second Platoon passed through this line and continued to advance with the Sherman tanks southward near the base of the ridge toward Turkey Knob.

Waller advanced carefully with two of his rifle squads in conjunction with the Sherman tanks. The Shermans crept slowly through the soft ash and torn terrain, pausing intermittently to fire at the blockhouse and other suspected positions on the ridge.

As the Sherman tank nearest Waller approached within twenty-five yards of the Knob, Japanese machine gun fire lashed out at the tank and nearby Marines from a position to the left front. The Sherman's seventy-five millimeter gun quickly neutralized this position, and Waller and his men moved to flank it. As they advanced, a second machine gun opened fire at close range from a concealed position nearby, killing one of the Marines. Japanese rifle fire now erupted from hidden positions in the ridge. Waller, less than fifty feet from the base of Turkey Knob, could see that no B Company Marines assigned to attack from the south were in sight.

Waller hand-signaled for his nearest squad leader to meet him at the rear of the Sherman and directed his young runner to cover them. As the runner took cover and brought his rifle to bear, a third hidden Japanese machine gun opened fire from the right front, killing him and wounding Waller's squad leader.

Dropping quickly behind the Sherman tank, Waller spotted one of the Japanese machine gunners and dispatched him with two shots from his carbine.

The tactical situation continued to deteriorate. Heavy mortar fire now joined the machine gun and rifle fire from positions in the ridge and Knob. Other Japanese hurled hand grenades, timing their throws to cause detonations as close as possible to Waller and his Marines behind cover provided by the Sherman.

This day's attack clearly had been stymied, and the enveloping B Company still was nowhere to be seen. Waller and the surviving members of his attacking squads managed to withdraw to the Third Platoon's supporting line, under cover of Ayresie's machine guns, and a fortuitous screen provided by clouds of volcanic ash and dust raised by the backing Shermans' powerful guns.

Only when his Marines and he had safely gained this position did Lieutenant Waller learn that B Company of 1/25 advancing from the south had come under heavy mortar fire, had taken heavy casualties, and was forced to withdraw before reaching Turkey Knob. The southern component of the enveloping pincer force had been eliminated, dooming the plan of attack.

For the next two days, I Company took up supporting positions in the Amphitheater and participated in mopping up isolated Japanese positions in the high ground and cliffs in that area.

A Marine under cover in the Amphitheater observes Turkey
Knob and the reinforced blockhouse, which appears to be under
attack by Marine engineers with Sherman tanks in support.

The continuing heavy casualties suffered by I Company and the entire Fourth Division were consistent with those suffered by the Fifth Division, advancing northward along Iwo Jima's western coast, and the Third Division, advancing adjacent to the Fourth in the center. Combat efficiency hovered at and below 50 percent in all units of the three Marine Divisions. Infantry companies normally led by captains now consisted of remnants led by junior or senior noncommissioned officers. Marines advancing in every part of the island were either being killed, wounded, or observing the deaths and injuries suffered by their comrades. The stubborn and disciplined Japanese resistance was taking a heavy toll. Yet, the Japanese defenders were dying at a greater rate than the Marines, and were suffering privation from lack of food and water. The uncaptured areas of the island were steadily diminishing as surviving Marines, in units diminished in number but not in courage, and with the aid of such armor and artillery support as could be effectively employed, attacked in small groups with rifles, machine guns, demolitions, and the ever-effective flame throwers.

Unit after unit in the Fourth Marine Division relieved each other in turn, and continued simultaneous attacks on the three elements of the Meat Grinder. Finally, by D plus thirteen, March 4, 1945, Hill 382 and Turkey Knob had fallen. Marines inspecting Hill 382 found that it held multiple subterranean chambers and was honeycombed by hundreds of yards of connecting passageways with multiple firing points. The Meat Grinder's defenses were far more intricate and extensive than had been anticipated.

The mopping up of organized resistance in the Amphitheater was concluded by D plus fourteen, March 5, 1945. The Twenty-Third Marines now was assigned responsibility for leading the attack to secure the remaining terrain extending to Iwo Jima's east coast. The regiment would attack beyond the Meat Grinder and advance in a southeastward direction. This direction of attack would coincide with the general direction of the torn and ragged ridges and ravines in this sector, reducing the need for more difficult "cross-compartment" attacks. Yet, the remaining ground over which the Twenty-Third Marines would fight still provided excellent cover and concealment to the fiercely resisting Japanese in the area.

To the Sea

On D plus fifteen, March 6, 1945, 3/23's I and K Companies assembled 400 yards to the north of Hill 382. At 0900 BLT 2/23 jumped off, followed in trace at a distance of 400 yards by I and K Companies. Japanese resistance by machine gun and rifle fire was heavy, but the day's advance had brought the Marines 350 yards closer to the coast of Iwo Jima near Tachiiwa Point.

The night of March 6 was active, with frequent exchanges of machine gun and rifle fire. Japanese approached the lines closely enough to hurl hand grenades at the Marine positions, but the positions held.

At noon on D plus sixteen, March 7, 1945, I Company was attached to 2/23, and with that battalion's E Company, advanced in line behind Companies G and F of 2/23 and Company K of 3-23.

On the following morning, D plus seventeen, March 8, 1945, the Third Battalion's Company K was relieved, and the front line units leading 2/23's assault southeastward toward the coast now consisted of, from left to right, G Company, Ayresie's I Company, and F Company. During the day's advance against stiff resistance, I Company reached a point slightly forward of G to its left and F to its right.

When 2/23's attack halted and formed defensive positions for the night of March 8, its front line positions formed an irregular curve facing southeast, and only some 900 yards from Iwo Jima's rocky eastern coast. A slight "bulge" forward in I Company's sector was held by Lieutenant Waller's Second Platoon and Ayresie's machine gun section. The companies remained in the same order as in the advance, with G, I, and F Companies, left to right. BLT 2/25's Company E was in a position to the right or southwest of Company F, leaving a gap of some two to three hundred yards where extremely rough terrain could not be effectively occupied and was covered by fire.

At the left boundary of Lieutenant Waller's and Ayresie's front line, a promontory overlooked lower ground to its front, giving way to more level terrain on the right where the Second Platoon's lines tied into those of F Company. This span was broad for defense by an understrength platoon, even with the support of Ayresie's well-placed machine guns. The Lieutenant received a few more inexperienced replacements to add to the unit's firepower in the event of a night attack.

Although numerous determined Japanese defenders clearly remained between the Marine lines and the sea, and Japanese riflemen and machine gunners still lurked in the nearby caves and ridges, the men of the composite 2/23 were in a strong defensive position for the night of March 8, 1945.

Counterattack

After eighteen days of bitter fighting against the costly but inexorable Marine advance, with American aviation and naval gunfire contributing all that they could, most of General Kuribayashi's communications from his headquarters near Kitano Point on Iwo Jima's northern coast to his subordinate commanders had been disrupted or destroyed. Some of these officers, thoroughly indoctrinated in the code of Bushido, had chafed from the very beginning under the general's standing orders to remain stationary in protected positions and kill as many American Marines as possible until dying themselves.

This anger and impatience was particularly felt by Samaji Inouye, a Japanese naval captain. As it happened, Captain Inouye commanded over 1,000 surviving Japanese troops in the area now immediately before 2/23 and I Company. The forty-nine year old officer was a fanatic. It was reported after the battle that he barely had been restrained from personally beheading Japanese soldiers who, in obedience to General Kuribayashi's specific orders, had avoided capture and managed to escape northward to other Japanese positions after Suribachi fell.

Captain Inouye may not have received communication from Kuribayashi for several days. For all he knew, the general might have been killed. As Inouye's frustration seethed and mounted on March 8, his determination to die for his emperor in a courageous attack eventually overcame his sense of discipline.

In addition, the eighth day of each month, adjusted for time zone differential, was observed by the Japanese military as a recurring monthly anniversary of the successful sneak attack on Pearl Harbor.

During the evening of March 8, only a few hundred yards forward of the defensive positions held by Lieutenant Waller, Ayresie, and the other Marines assigned to 2/23, Captain Inouye assembled all troops remaining under his command and issued his orders for a strong night attack against the American lines.

This was not to be a suicidal banzai attack in its initial stages. Captain Inouye's orders were to approach silently, and then to attack and carry through the Marine lines to destroy American aircraft and forces on Airfield One. If successful to this point, the surviving Japanese were ordered to continue to destroy all Americans in their path, reoccupy Mount Suribachi, and raise the Rising Sun flag in place of the American flag that had flown at its summit since February 23.

As darkness fell, Japanese mortar and rocket fire began to fall in and around the Marine lines. Soon, although no screams erupted as in previous Japanese attacks on other islands, the Marines of Lieutenant Waller's Second Platoon and others all along 2/23's lines heard sounds of movement to their front.

Inouye's men, armed with all the remaining weapons they could muster, crept quietly toward the Americans. Captain Inouye led, waving his sword and quietly exhorting his troops.

The Japanese carried rifles, light machine guns or grenades, and some salvaged American weapons. Many wore Marine utilities. Others strapped explosive mines to their bodies to detonate them among the Marines. A determined few were armed with nothing more than poles with their tips sharpened into makeshift spears.

When the Japanese had closed with the Marine positions, they rose and charged, firing their weapons and throwing grenades and spears as they came. Some Japanese bearing stretchers retrieved from the battlefield called out in fair imitation of English, "Corpsman! Corpsman!"

The attack struck heavily at the gap between F and E Companies, but all the units in 2/23's defense line were hit, including I Company.

From the promontory at the left of the Second Platoon's positions, Private First Class Walter Berry, whose position provided an excellent field of fire, steadily fired his BAR at the attacking Japanese. He was joined in his foxhole by a young replacement, also so armed. From nearby, the controlled bursts of Ayresie's machine gun crews also engaged the attackers.

All along the lines the attacking Japanese, lit by illumination shells from Marine mortars and naval vessels offshore, were falling, but more came on. Several penetrated within a few yards of Colonel Dillon's Second Battalion command post, but the Marines fought furiously and well, and the lines held or were quickly restored.

From the Second Platoon's position, the Marines kept up a disciplined and steady fire against the Japanese assaulting their positions, now no longer silent, and loudly screaming "Banzai."

Since childhood, Ayresie had quickly stepped, or more accurately, sprung forward whenever a critical need arose. This decisive leadership trait was recognized and rewarded by the Marine Corps, contributing to his promotions to corporal and sergeant, and to his assignment as a machine gun section leader, just over two years following his graduation from boot camp.

As an expert rifleman and experienced machine gunner, Ayresie knew that the steady firing by his Machine gunners and by the BAR men on the promontory was depleting their ammunition supplies. Two men had already been wounded while attempting to resupply I Company Marines in their frontline positions. Ayresie was also aware that I Company Marines had reported concerns about Japanese occupying a cave on or near the promontory.

Gathering several loaded BAR magazines and some demolitions for use in sealing the caves if needed, Ayresie began to hurry in a crouching run up the slope of the promontory where the ammunition and charges were needed. Mortar rounds and rockets continued to explode in the area, and shots rang out in the darkness, but Ayresie continued to struggle upward with his vital load. Suddenly, he dropped to the ground, the magazines and explosives he carried scattering down the slope.

Walter Berry quickly hurried to Ayresie's side, but he lay still and lifeless. The favorite son of Montrose, and the experienced and respected Marine NCO who had fought in and survived the battles of Roi-Namur, Saipan, Tinian, and eighteen days of the Marine Corps' bloodiest battle of the Pacific campaign, was gone.

Like other survivors of the bitter, grinding battle to capture Iwo Jima, the Marines of Second Platoon, I Company could only fight back tears or wipe them from their grimy faces, curse in angry frustration, and cover Ayresie's body with his poncho for eventual removal to the Fourth Marine Division cemetery. They had lost not only a brave, competent, and respected leader, but also a cherished comrade, for Ayresie was one of the rare breed of leaders who naturally earn both the respect and affection of subordinates. Lieutenant Waller wrote to his own family days later aboard the transport returning 3/23's survivors to Maui,

> "This was a great loss. It was felt throughout the company. He had been a big brother to many of the men and was my platoon sergeant's best friend. He had always done more than his share regardless of the danger. It was indeed a blow."

Hallowed Ground

The careful and respectful treatment of Ayresie and other Marines killed on Iwo Jima may have been of limited comfort to, or just as likely unknown by their families and loved ones, but it deserves mention here.

Months before the invasion, location of cemeteries on Iwo Jima for all three Marine divisions participating in Operation Detachment had been carefully planned north of Mount Suribachi and inland from the invasion beaches. Supply vessels in the invasion fleet carried thousands of preassembled grave markers bearing crosses and Stars of David.

The heavy stream of Marines killed in action on Iwo Jima challenged burial details, but the challenge was met. Burials were well organized and respectful, even as occasional Japanese artillery or mortar rounds fell in the immediate area.

Ayresie was laid out in the same Marine dungarees and boondockers he wore as he climbed the high ground on the left of the Second Platoon's lines. His identity was carefully confirmed and reconfirmed by his identification or "dog" tag. His body remained wrapped in the poncho that had covered him since he fell. His serviceable weapon, helmet, and field gear, including the new canteen he was issued following his escape from LST 69 in Pearl Harbor, were collected as battle salvage.

Bulldozers had plowed long, straight rows four to six feet deep in Iwo Jima's sandy and ashy soil. Extreme rigor was employed to identify and bury each Marine in a precisely designated and accurately recorded place within a row. Before each Marine was laid to rest, his body was fingerprinted if possible, as in Ayresie's case. One of his two ID tags was kept on or with his body. Chaplains of Christian and Jewish faiths accompanied the Marines tasked with laying each body to rest. A Protestant chaplain spoke and prayed over Ayresie.

Above each man's body a simple wood marker bearing his name, service number, and service emblem—a Marine's eagle, globe, and anchor for Ayresie, or a naval symbol for corpsmen— was carefully placed. When a row was fully occupied, it was filled and covered with a layer of clay to stabilize the soil. The preplaced markers were then secured to the ground in their proper positions, and low, raised berms were formed over the graves.

Every Marine buried on Iwo Jima lay a precisely measured distance from those to his left and right. Ayresie lay this distance from two other Marines, one spoken over and buried just before him; the other just after. Even in death, Marines who gave their lives on Iwo Jima took their positions and lay in formation.

As any who have seen or attended a United States Marine's military funeral service know, the Marine Corps takes care of its own, living and dead.

Fourth Marine Division Marines search for their buddies after dedication of the division cemetery. One Marine has found his.

The Battle Concludes

The attack of Inouye and his remaining troops during the night of March 8 and early morning of March 9 had claimed Ayresie's life and that of some eighty other Marines. It also had cost the lives of almost all of the remaining and organized Japanese troops in the Fourth Division's sector. Over 800 Japanese dead were found before the Fourth Division lines on March 9 and 10.

By March 11, I Company had attacked through rugged coastal ravines, taking light casualties against pockets of Japanese resistance, and had reached Tachiiwa Point and the sea. Its assigned area was essentially secure, and its active combat mission completed.

Over the next few days, Fourth Division Marines policed the area they had seized at such cost. Any uncollected bodies of American Marines or corpsmen were marked for retrieval. "Policing" included the burial of dead Japanese, either individually or in common graves where groups were found.

On March 16, 1945, D plus twenty-five, the Twenty-Third Marines assembled on Yellow Beach One, and began to be ferried to their transports for the return to Maui. Lieutenant Hawk Waller, Private First Class Walter Berry, and "Ski" Rutkowski were among just over one hundred surviving members of I Company who were capable of walking aboard APA 177, the USS Kingsbury, for the return voyage to Maui. Including replacements, almost 400 Marines had served in I Company on Iwo Jima. The balance, nearly 300 Marines, had been killed, seriously wounded, or were listed as missing, a euphemism applied to those whose bodies were obliterated or unrecoverable, in some cases buried in the volcanic sands by explosions or sealed in Japanese caves or tunnels. Truly missing.

The Fourth Marine Division had spent itself taking Airfields One and Two, and securing what most describe as the most difficult and deadly portion of Iwo Jima. The division would regroup, reorganize, and train at Camp Maui, but it would never fight again in World War II.

The Fifth Division on the west, and the Third Division in the center, also had fought tough and deadly battles northward over deadly ground and against equally determined and fanatically committed Japanese defenders.

The Fifth Division's Twenty-Eighth Marines landed on Green Beach, crossed the island at its narrowest point, and took Mount Suribachi. The Twenty-Seventh Marines landed just to the north and fought to the northeast, assuming the western portion of the northward advance. The Fifth Division's battle history includes costly battles for spurred and tunneled Hill 362A, Nishi Ridge, and Hill 372B. On March 23, the division took General Kuribayashi's final cave headquarters, and on March 25, with the assistance of elements of the Third Division, snuffed out all organized Japanese resistance in "Bloody Gorge," a 700-yard ravine teeming with protected firing positions and opening to the sea.

The Third Division, initially afloat in reserve, landed one of its three regiments, the Twenty-First Marines, on D plus three to the left of the Fourth Division sector, and a second, the Ninth Marines, two days later. These Third Division regiments fought northward between the Fifth Division on their left and the Fourth Division on their right over the high ground of the Motoyama Plateau, including Hills 362 B and C. Third Division troops captured the third and northernmost airfield, reduced "Cushman's Pocket," and reached the north central coast. Enthusiastic Third Division Marines sent a canteen of seawater from the limit of their advance to General Schmidt with a message of caution to the V Corps Commander: "For inspection, not consumption."

On the day following Ayresie's death in the Fourth Division's sector, Marines of the Third Division had taken the cliffs above the seashore in its zone. That day, March 9, 1945, also saw hundreds of loaded B-29 bombers lift off from runways on Saipan and Tinian where Ayresie had fought the previous summer, and launch massive and devastating incendiary bomb attacks on Tokyo, destroying sixteen square miles of the capital city and some 100,000 of its inhabitants.

In all three division sectors, the final drive to take Iwo Jima required Marine Corps units, most reduced to less than 50 percent combat efficiency and with a steadily increasing percentage of inexperienced replacements, to fight at close range and often hand-to-hand through torn and rocky ravines and ridges against a fanatical enemy resisting to the very last. In these latter stages, and although armed as usual with their individual weapons, flamethrowers, and demolitions, the Marines' proximity to the enemy often deprived them of close artillery, naval gunfire, or air support.

On March 16, 1945, Iwo Jima was officially declared secure. General Schmidt and many other senior naval and

Marine Corps officers had departed on March 14 and were now fully committed to the upcoming invasion and capture of Okinawa, the final island stepping stone to Japan itself.

On the same day the cemeteries for the Third, Fourth, and Fifth Divisions were dedicated. Stirring words were spoken by division commanders and by a Jewish chaplain. Major General Graves Erskine, Commander of the Third Marine Division, spoke succinctly and eloquently of his Marines who had died taking the central portion of the island.

> "Victory was never in doubt. Its cost was. What was in doubt in all our minds was whether there would be any of us left to dedicate our cemetery at the end, or whether the last Marine would die knocking out the last Japanese gunner."

The General's unspoken question was a fair one.

The battle for Iwo Jima is generally regarded as lasting thirty-six days from February 19 to March 26, 1945, although US Army garrison troops on Iwo Jima continued to search out stragglers for many months, killing hundreds more Japanese. On the battle's "final day," March 26, 1945, as the Twenty-Third Marines sailed toward their Pacific base on Maui, some 300 surviving Japanese crawled from their caves and gathered in the predawn darkness in the northwestern section of the island. The assembled troops silently crept southward along an obscure path fringing the west coast. Their objective was a bivouac area near Airfield

Two occupied by US Army Air Corps pilots and Marine Corps service troops. The area was considered as secure as any on the island.

Many of the Japanese were officers and senior NCOs, as later determined by their being armed with swords. Others carried a variety of American BARs, M1 rifles, or .45 pistols taken from dead Marines. Again, some wore Marine Corps utilities.

Just before dawn this group fell upon the sleeping American pilots in their tents, slashing and killing with their swords, throwing grenades, and firing their weapons. Explosions, shots, and screams alerted sleeping US Navy Armed Construction Battalion men or "Seabees," shore party Marines, and other ground troops. A pitched battle quickly ensued, with shots and grenade explosions filling the darkness. A unit of disciplined Marine pioneer troops, led by First Lieutenant Harry Martin, formed a defense line, halted the Japanese attack against their position, and then counter-attacked.

This last organized Japanese attack on Iwo Jima failed. Two-hundred Twenty-three Japanese were killed, 196 in the Marine pioneer unit's area. Forty-four American fighter pilots were killed, and eighty-eight were wounded. The Marine pioneer unit lost thirty-one wounded and nine killed. Among those killed was Lieutenant Martin, who received a posthumous Medal of Honor, the last of thirty-six awarded to Americans fighting on Iwo Jima.

Almost 6,000 US Marines died instantly or succumbed from their wounds in the battle for Iwo Jima. For the first time in the Pacific War, total Marine casualties of 25,851 killed and wounded surpassed the total casualties suffered by the estimated 22,000 Japanese defending the island. However, virtually all Japanese casualties were killed in action, including General Kuribayashi, whose body was never recovered. Only 216 prisoners were taken by Marines by March 26, and almost all of them were Korean laborers. Although total Marine casualties exceeded those suffered by Iwo Jima's defenders, the 6,000 Marine dead and their surviving comrades had wiped out the Japanese garrison on Iwo Jima and had accomplished their mission with courage and honor.

Return and Deliverance

Aboard the *Kingsbury*, Lieutenant Waller, Private First Class Berry, and Ski Rutkowski rested with the other survivors of 3/23, showered, and were well fed by sympathetic messmen in the ship's galley during the return voyage from Iwo Jima to Maui.

As the *Kingsbury* docked in Kahului Harbor, the Marines aboard received an enthusiastic welcome. A band, crowds, and hula dancers lined the dock. A large hanging banner assured the returning Marines, "You bet we're happy you are back." Cheering crowds along the road from the harbor to Camp Maui smiled, some extending refreshments and flowers to the passing troops.

On arrival at Camp Maui, the mood became more somber and restrained. Iwo Jima had winnowed all units that fought there. Tom Savery, who had recovered and rejoined I Company at Camp Maui, recognized Ski among the returning Marines. Tom found him changed from the gruff but smiling man who had urged him to leap from the burning deck of LST 69 into the West Loch of Pearl Harbor, and who two months before had joined Ayresie in bidding him farewell at Aiea Heights Naval Hospital. Ski was now morose and withdrawn. Given the loss of close friends of all ranks, this was understandable.

As the First and Sixth Marine Divisions, aided by the Second Marine Division, and by four US Army divisions, fought yet another bloody and costly battle for the island of Okinawa, the Fourth Marine Division resumed the cycle of restoring all units to full strength and training for the largest invasion of all: Operation Downfall, the invasion of the Japanese home islands. Plans were already near completion for this massive operation that would commence in November of 1945 with the invasion of the southernmost island, Kyushu. Throughout the Pacific, the assigned units prepared for a pitched, deadly, and lengthy battle. Based on the intractable strategy of Japanese attrition displayed at Peleliu, Iwo Jima, and finally at Okinawa, the scope of the battle to conquer the entire Japanese nation, defended by desperate and fanatical military personnel and civilians alike, was almost beyond comprehension. Projected American casualties for the entire operation ran into the millions, with estimated Japanese casualties well in excess of that figure. Sardonic Marines echoed a grim and possibly optimistic slogan for those who might survive: "The Golden Gate in Forty-Eight."

Both adversary nations were spared this unimaginable fight to the death when Japan unconditionally surrendered following the dropping of atomic bombs on the cities of Hiroshima and Nagasaki in August of 1945.

Epilogue to Detachment

The US War Department's telegram advising Ayresie's father that he had been killed in action on Iwo Jima did not arrive until April 26, 1945. Word of his death quickly spread through the community.

On Sunday, April 29, 1945, a memorial service for Ayresie was held at the Montrose Presbyterian Church, which Harriette and he had attended, and where they likely would have been married had he survived for three more days until the Twenty-Third Marines were relieved of their active combat role in the Fourth Division's sector of Iwo Jima. At the conclusion of the memorial service, Harriette tearfully returned to Ayresie's parents the engagement ring he had bought in North Carolina., and had given to her in Montrose on his Christmas leave.

The *Susquehanna Independent* ran a front page article reporting Ayresie's death on Iwo Jima complete with his military portrait in uniform. Following a short history of his birth, high school graduation, and military service, the article expressed the entire community's "...deep sympathy in the loss of a young man so generally loved and admired."

During October of 1945, units of the Fourth Marine Division boarded transports and sailed from Maui for San Diego, California. The Fourth Division Marines arrived over a period of three to four weeks, and on November 28, 1945, the Fourth Marine Division was formally deactivated. Through the Roi-Namur, Saipan, Tinian, and Iwo Jima campaigns, the division had suffered 17,722 casualties, with 3,298 men killed in action or dying of wounds and 14,424 wounded. The Fourth Marine Division was awarded two presidential unit citations. Its members earned eight Medals of Honor, 111 Navy Crosses, four Distinguished Service Medals, 646 Silver Stars, 53 Legions of Merit, 36 Distinguished Flying Crosses, 57 Navy-Marine Corps Medals, 2,517 Bronze Stars, 103 Air Medals, and 14,736 Purple Hearts.

During 1946 and 1947, special units returned to Iwo Jima and carefully exhumed for repatriation the remains of all Marines and other servicemen buried in the division cemeteries on Iwo Jima. All buried remains, including some that had fallen into collapsed Japanese tunnels below, were recovered and prepared for reburial. Each Marine's identity was confirmed not only by location, but also by the identification tag buried with his body. The same repatriation process occurred in US Marine cemeteries on other islands taken in the Pacific, including Saipan and Tinian.

Predesignated family members received a single notice providing a choice between two options for reburial of their loved one's remains. The remains either could be returned to the United States for burial by their family or personal representative, or buried in an undesignated "American military cemetery overseas." Bob Avery's family opted for the return of his remains, and they are buried in a cemetery near his hometown in New York.

Ayresie's father decided to elect the overseas military cemetery option. Ayresie's remains, like others whose families chose the overseas option for their loved ones buried on Iwo Jima, are interred at the National Military Cemetery of the Pacific, the beautiful and famous "Punchbowl." There were exceptions. A number of Marines killed at Iwo Jima are buried at Arlington National Cemetery, including "Manila John" Basilone and Iwo Jima flag raisers Mike Strank, Ira Hayes, and Rene Gagnon.

Tom Savery and William "Ski" Rutkowski returned to their homes in New York and Pennsylvania, married and raised children, and enjoyed quiet careers in civilian life. Their memories of combat in the Pacific never left them.

Walter Berry, promoted to corporal before his release from active duty, returned to his Illinois hometown and married his sweetheart, Eva Jane Branson, whose picture he had carried with him on Iwo Jima. Walter lived a full and happy life with his wife and children, but was frequently disturbed by his memories of combat on Iwo Jima.

Lieutenant Harcourt Waller, who earned a Bronze Star on Iwo Jima and was later promoted to captain, returned to Georgia, met and married Kathryn Johnson, and became a respected, ordained Episcopal minister. He and his wife raised a family of four children. Always a loyal Marine, Reverend Waller sometimes enlivened sermons to his parishioners with his Marine Corps experiences, including some in combat.

Millions of Americans celebrated "VJ Day" on August 15, 1945. Joyous crowds thronged in every city, town, and hamlet. Others would continue to grieve the loss of their fathers, husbands, sons, and brothers. Tom Savery's brother was killed in action in Normandy within one week of Tom's being wounded on Saipan, prompting him to say that, "Mom had a tough time that week."

Ayresie and Bob Avery did not live to reunite in the New York and Pennsylvania borderlands they loved, or to marry and enjoy good and full lives with their wives and families. Their lives ended in an instant, less than nine months apart on Saipan and Iwo Jima. Bob and Ayresie no doubt were justifiably proud to be United States Marines. One expects that they also felt pride in having bravely faced the greatest threats that human experience can provide. Like thousands of others, they gave their lives for their Marine buddies and their country.

No epitaph appears on Bob Avery's gravestone in New York, or on Ayresie's marker at the Punchbowl on Oahu; only their names, service branch, and rank, the outfit in which they served, and the war-shortened span of their lives. There should be more; some simple statement they earned by giving their last, full measure of devotion in furious battle.

I suggest the words composed by Marine combat veteran and author Robert Leckie for his comrades lost in the Pacific campaign. From his *Helmet for My Pillow*:

> "...There are no glorious living, but only glorious dead. Heroes turn traitor, warriors age and grow soft—but a victim is changeless, sacrifice is eternal."

CHAPTER 11

IRISH PENNANTS

Marine Corps service uniforms and dungarees, particularly during boot training and preparation for inspections, are closely scrutinized by drill instructors determined at all costs to instill strict discipline and attention to detail. Any flaw or imperfection, even a single dangling thread, is assailed as an "Irish Pennant," resulting in a good chewing out, at least. That phrase, whose origin has been traced to the 19th century British Navy, is used here as a traditional component of the lexicon of the United States Marine Corps to describe loose ends or unfinished business. No disrespect to the Irish or anyone of Irish descent is in the least intended.

Ayresie's Death on Iwo Jima

The most significant unresolved issue I must address involves my eventual discovery of three distinct and separately reported versions of the cause and manner of Ayresie's death during the Japanese attack from the late evening of March 8 to the early morning hours of March 9, 1945.

The earliest description of Ayresie's death that I received appeared in his posthumous Bronze Star citation with combat

V. In the stentorian language of combat decorations, the citation stated:

> For heroic achievement as a Section Leader of Company I, Third Battalion, Twenty-Third Marines, Fourth Marine Division, during action against enemy Japanese forces on Iwo Jima, Volcano Islands, on 8 March 1945. Skillfully deploying his men in a defensive position at dusk, Sergeant Ayres braved the intense enemy machine-gun and sniper fire to guide men bringing supplies to all positions of his platoon and by his determined efforts obtained ammunition, rations and demolitions for the night. Undertaking a last mission across the platoon front after two Marines had been wounded in attempting the trip, he was struck down by the hostile barrage. His indomitable fighting spirit and self-sacrificing action on behalf of his men reflect the highest credit upon Sergeant Ayres and the United States Naval Service. He gallantly gave his life for his country.
>
> For the President,
>
> /s/ John L. Sullivan
>
> Secretary of the Navy.

This description is consistent with Ayresie's official casualty report, which states that his mortal wounds were caused by "FRAG shell Back." That report also squares with the Japanese mortar and rocket fire indisputably falling on I

Company's position before and during Captain Inouye's night attack and with his citation's statement that Ayresie was "struck down by the hostile barrage."

Case closed. However, months later, I learned of a second account of Ayresie's death. An online search using "Harris C. Ayres, Jr." produced a startling article quoting a remark by an Iwo Jima veteran—none other than Private First Class Walter Berry of Belleville, Illinois. Berry returned home following his discharge from the Marine Corps. Later, during interviews through the Veteran's History Project, the aging Marine veteran was quoted as having said that his "worst memory" of Iwo Jima was the "death of Sergeant Harris Ayres."

This quotation led to my contacting Mrs. Eva Jane Berry, Walter's widow. Mrs. Berry generously furnished me a copy of Walter's carefully written and illustrated "Life Story," which included his description of service with the Second Platoon, I Company on Iwo Jima.

Berry's written version of events on the night of March 8, 1945, which was reinforced by my discussions with the Belleville, Illinois news reporter who personally interviewed him on several occasions, held that as Ayresie mounted the high ground on the left of the Second Platoon's position to resupply his comrades atop the promontory, an inexperienced Marine replacement sharing Berry's foxhole mistook Ayresie in the darkness for a stealthily approaching Japanese. The replacement panicked and shot Ayresie with a burst from his Browning automatic rifle, killing him instantly. Berry stated that he had yelled at the replacement, "Do you know what you have done? You've just killed Sergeant Ayres!" The despairing replacement collapsed with grief, sobbed for hours in the foxhole, and was relieved of duty the following morning.

According to Private Berry, given the respect and affection all in the platoon felt for Ayresie, neither he nor anyone else in a position to report details of his death could conceive of informing his family and fiancée that he was killed by friendly fire.

As a sobering footnote to Private Berry's account, the reporter who had interviewed him revealed to me another statement by Berry, which was not included in his recorded interviews.

Berry customarily enjoyed lingering on deck after nightfall aboard his troopship and admiring from its stern the bright phosphorescence created by the ship's wake. Berry was so engaged aboard the *Kingsbury* one night as it steamed toward Maui. As he gazed downward over the stern rail, a "huge Polish Marine" loomed out of the darkness and confronted him. The Marine, standing closely beside Berry, quietly uttered, "Tell me the name of the cook who shot Ayres, or you're going over the side."

This Marine almost certainly was William "Ski" Rutkowski. Ski apparently had not served in Ayresie's machine gun section on March 8 or 9, and only recently had heard a rumor that friendly fire by an unidentified replacement cook had killed his close friend.

Private Berry, who fought with courage and skill throughout his first combat experience on Iwo Jima, had the good sense to dissemble and to express ignorance and disbelief of this report. If Ski meant what he said, and the plainspoken Marine had not been known to bluff, Berry's response saved not only his own life, but also that of Ski, who was infuriated to hear that his close friend had died in such a needless manner. Corporal Berry's description of this episode aboard the *Kingsbury* is revealed here in print for the first time.

Finally, yet a third description of Sergeant Ayres' death emerged.

Lieutenant Harcourt Waller, the Commander of Second Platoon, I Company, passed away in 1989. His widow, Kathryn Waller, shared with me her late husband's detailed journal, written aboard the *Kingsbury* very shortly after it departed Iwo Jima for the return voyage to Maui. Lieutenant Waller, whose expression of sadness and respect for his brave "machine gun sergeant" appears elsewhere in this book, wrote that as Ayresie began to climb the promontory carrying ammunition and explosives, he was shot and killed by a Japanese sniper.

All known eyewitnesses to Ayresie's death, including Lieutenant Waller, Corporal Berry, and even the unfortunate cook assigned to I Company on the night of March 8, 1945, have passed away.

Where lies the truth? As a trial lawyer in civilian life, my initial instinct was to weigh the evidence and analyze factors that might militate for or against the reliability of each version of this tragic event. There are such factors. For example, Lieutenant Waller's account was prepared mere days after Ayresie's death and has the advantage of having been prepared contemporaneously with the event. Corporal Berry's written account was made years later and lacks the advantage of close proximity in time. Yet, its sincerity and consistency are compelling. Both men unquestionably lived out their lives as reputable, well-respected citizens.

The noble language of Ayresie's official Bronze Star citation also rings true, and is supported by action reports and by his official Marine Corps casualty report.

Enough. Such analyses and comparisons are futile. The truth is that no dishonor attends any of these separate accounts or their sources. Nor should criticism be directed toward each version's authors or reported perpetrators, whether some Japanese riflemen or mortarman fighting Americans to the last as ordered, the unfortunate Marine replacement who may honestly have mistaken Ayresie in the heat of combat for a Japanese soldier, or any Marines of I Company, officer or enlisted, who either accurately reported the manner of Ayresie's death or concluded in their hearts that, given his unflinching courage and dedication, a report to loved ones that his death was inflicted by friendly fire mere days before the end of I Company's fight to the sea should not be endured.

The true details of Ayresie's death now are known only to God, or perhaps by some skilled Japanese rifleman who was among the few Japanese survivors on Iwo Jima, and who by the slimmest of chances lives to this day. In any event, those details, even if they could conclusively be confirmed, are irrelevant. Sergeant Harris C. Ayres, Jr. gave his life in combat while doing his duty and taking an obvious risk called for by a pressing combat emergency. Ayresie no more could have remained passively under cover when his fellow Marines needed ammunition or explosives in the midst of a banzai attack than he could have killed them himself. Whatever the precise cause of his death, Ayresie gallantly gave his life for his country.

Betty

What of Betty, Ayresie's intended recipient of news if he did not "make it back?"

"Tell Betty," the final phrase of Ayresie's scratched message on his canteen, tugged immediately and strongly at the heartstrings of all who saw or heard of it. Its emotional appeal prompted my inquiries from Pennsylvania, southward to North Carolina and Georgia, and westward to the Hawaiian islands. None bore fruit.

Harriette Whitney Crooks (nee Weston) was certain that her beloved fiancé had remained as steadfastly faithful to her as she had to him. Ayresie was a handsome, charismatic, young man, but he deserved her trust. This fact is confirmed by his buddies, living and dead, who eagerly sought the pleasures of liberty in North Carolina and Southern California, while Ayresie remained at Camp Lejeune and Camp Pendleton. The couple's engagement ended only when word of his death reached Montrose, Pennsylvania, and Harriette.

Thus, no evidence of any short-lived wartime romance, other than that of Harris and Harriette in Susquehanna County, ever emerged or can be asserted with any support. Who, then, was Betty? By process of elimination, I have arrived at what I believe to be the most likely answer.

Conversations with surviving Marine veterans who fought in the Pacific revealed that a phrase whose frequent use rivaled "Kilroy was here" arose from what is generally considered the most popular and widely distributed World War II pinup photograph of all time.

The phrase, "Tell Betty," was the equivalent of "So what," "Call someone who cares," or the appropriately more vulgar, "Tough shit." World War II Marines, soldiers, and sailors hearing some pointless gripe often would state dismissively, "Tell Betty." Use of the phrase in this manner, especially in the event Ayresie were not to "make it back," was entirely typical of his tough attitude, and a sense of humor and irony that never left him. It was quite like Ayresie to taunt his uncertain fate in this way.

To seal or at least to lend further support to my conclusion, correspondence from Bob Avery, enclosing an illustrated news article, established that Ayresie and he attended and were entertained by the subject of the phrase in a live performance at Camp Lejeune in late 1942.

"Betty," in my opinion, was none other than Betty Grable, she of the "million dollar legs," who smiled fetchingly backward over her shoulder at World War II US Marines, soldiers, and sailors everywhere, both improving their morale, and in her own innocent yet provocative way, beckoning them homeward.

I acknowledge that my conclusion certainly must quash the romantic notion of a loving Betty waiting at home for her brave warrior to return. Early in this project, and well before I heard of this retort commonly used by World War II servicemen, I imagined a wife or wartime lover whom Ayresie was determined should receive word if he failed to survive Iwo Jima. Yet, as my research through interviews and other means progressed, and I came to know and appreciate Ayresie's character, courage, devotion to duty, and the high esteem in which he was held by his fellow Marines, his fiancée, and his entire home town, the life and service of Marine Sergeant Harris C. Ayres, Jr. became the central and compelling story that deserved to be told.

Betty

ACKNOWLEDGMENTS

I owe a personal debt of thanks to many who have assisted me in launching and completing this labor of loyalty and love for the United States Marine Corps, and for each one of the thousands of US Marines, some recognized officially for their bravery and others not, who fought and conquered the Japanese Empire in the Pacific Island campaign.

First, to my beloved wife and partner, Sharon, who faithfully accompanied me for hundreds of miles up and down the eastern seaboard, as we met and interviewed veterans who served with Harris Ayres, and others who were his close friends. Sharon also typed and corrected multiple drafts of my manuscript as I struggled to get this Marine's story right.

My fellow US Marine and good friend, Delmar Lee Reynolds, saved and passed Sergeant Harris Ayres' canteen to me and with it the privilege of learning and telling his story. Lee's encouragement, and his advice as a published author in his own right, were constant catalysts as the tasks of research and other work mounted.

Several fine residents of Montrose, Pennsylvania shared with me their strong memories of Ayresie and the photographs and memorabilia they had preserved for over sixty years. Norville, Delbert, and Elizabeth Potts and their significant others spent days with us recalling the happy times they spent with Ayresie after he was welcomed into their home and hearts. Harriette Weston Crooks also joined us during our visit to Montrose and spoke fondly of Ayresie, and the couple's courtship and engagement. Harriette loaned me the original photographs of Ayresie and her in the summer of 1942, as well as others that Ayresie, then a young machine gunner, took and personally inscribed for her at Camp Lejeune.

Mrs. Lori Lass, English teacher at Harris' alma mater, shared my enthusiasm for Ayresie's story, and arranged meetings and contacts with Ayresie's classmates and other Montrose residents whom I never would have located, much less met and spoken with at length, without her unselfish assistance.

The officers and members of VFW Post 5642, the Ayres-Stone Post, welcomed us to Montrose and gave me Ayresie's official Purple Heart citation and other records, as well as the official photograph taken just after he received the decoration on Maui. That photograph forms part of the front cover of this book. I was deeply moved by their gift to me of the very same American flag that draped Ayresie's coffin for his reburial with honors at the National Memorial Cemetery of the Pacific on Oahu. This flag occupies a place of honor in our home.

Frank Niader of Clifton, New Jersey has embarked on a number of tasks in honor of his older brother, nineteen-year-old US Marine Private Bill Niader, who was killed in action at Okinawa's Kunishi Ridge. Those tasks have become a philanthropic second career, in which Frank skillfully has used several sources to provide hundreds of families of deceased veterans information about their loved ones, often enabling them to contact survivors who fought with them. In this manner, Frank helped me locate and identify several veterans or surviving relatives of veterans who knew and served with Ayresie.

The dedicated workers at the National Archives in College Park, Maryland, acted as pathfinders by retrieving and organizing in advance of my scheduled arrival a wealth of official operation reports of Ayresie's Twenty-Third Marines and its subordinate units, down to the company and platoon levels.

Robert Aquilinas of the Marine Corps Historical Branch in Quantico, Virginia, assisted me on numerous occasions by obtaining official Marine Corps casualty reports, and muster rolls of the Twenty-Third Marines for the Saipan, Tinian, and Iwo Jima invasions.

The National Personnel Records Center in St. Louis, Missouri, provided copies of Ayresie's personnel record and those of others in his squad.

Chattanoogan Steve McCloud, although not technically a US Marine, has thoroughly researched the Marine Corps' battles in the Pacific, as well as Marine Corps training methods, tactics, and traditions. Steve has adapted Marine Corps philosophy and principles of task organization and leadership in a successful career, teaching these principles to civilian organizations and others. His work and commitment to the Marine Corps have so impressed World War II Marines that he has been designated an official, honorary member of F Company, Twenty-Third Marines, whose position flanked that of Ayresie's I Company on the night of March 8, 1945. In the course of his extensive research, including multiple visits to Saipan, Tinian and Iwo Jima, Steve has compiled a collection of official reports and photographs about the Fourth Division in World War II that rivals any I have seen. He unselfishly shared these reports, photographs, and information personally provided by veterans who fought in Operations Forager and Detachment. Steve's accurate sketch maps of the four Pacific objections taken by the Fourth Marine Division add clarity to the narrative of the Twenty-Third Marines' advances in those operations.

Veterans and Their Relatives

Several Marines who carried their personal memories of the Pacific war all their lives willingly shared them directly with me and often experienced renewed agony in the telling. To them, I give my profound thanks and my sincere respect. Some are:

First Lieutenant Charles Ahern, Executive Officer, F Company, 23rd Marines

Corporal William B. Allen, thirty-seven millimeter anti-tank gunner, 23rd Marines

Corporal John A. Minnella, machine gun section leader, K Company, 23rd Marines

Sergeant "Iron Mike" Mervosh, machine gun section leader, 24th Marines

Corporal Charles Garabedian, K Company, 23rd Marines

Corporal Ed Marthens, 25th Marines

Corporal Ralph Leinoff, machine gun squad leader, F Company, 23rd Marines

Private Roy Stewart, machine gunner, F Company, 23rd Marines

Private Jack Simms, machine gunner, F Company, 23rd Marines

Surviving family members of other Marines who served with Ayresie shared their own cherished loved ones' written words with me. Marine muster rolls disclosed the name of Lieutenant Harcourt Waller, who led the Second Platoon of I Company from D plus five for the balance of Operation Detachment. That information led me to Kathryn Waller, who shared Hawk Waller's extensively detailed and contemporary hand-written report to his family about his daily participation with Ayresie and others in the battle for Iwo Jima, as well as the photograph of Lieutenant Waller in Honolulu that appears in this book. But for Kathryn's generosity, far more of my account of Ayresie's experiences within those deadly eight square miles would have been the product only of official reports.

Through Mrs. Lori Lass' assistance, I was able to contact and speak at length with Corporal Robert Avery's sister, Mrs. Lee Culley of Colorado. After learning of my project and receiving for the first time a credible account of the exact date and manner of her brother's death on Saipan, Lee sent me copies of Bob's extensive, well-written correspondence with members of the Avery family. In these letters, Bob gave many details of his close friendship and experiences with Ayresie, dating from their New York enlistment through the Marshall and Marianas Island campaigns.

My final acknowledgment is to Tom Savery, Ayresie's number one machine gunner. Proudly sporting a faded red baseball cap bearing the Fourth Marine Division patch, Tom welcomed Sharon and me to his small, squared-away Pennsylvania home. On his wall was a copy of Joe Rosenthal's famous photograph of the February 23, 1945 Mount Suribachi flag raising. In his carefully kept garden flew a small Marine Corps flag.

Tom spent days with us. Still alert and erect though well into his eighties, he spent hours discussing his friendship, training, and service with Ayresie, Bob Avery, and William Rutkowski. He relived the invasion of Roi-Namur, his reluctant leap from LST 69 into the flaming waters of the West Loch of Pearl Harbor, the bloody Saipan landing, and the other terrible events of June 15, 1944. Tom did us the honor of becoming our friend.

As I left his home for the last time, Tom described how Iwo Jima had decimated his squad and his small circle of close friends assembling at Camp Maui, deeply saddening them all. The lingering pain of those memories was visibly apparent. As we said our farewells, Tom turned and looked westward from his garden toward a Pennsylvania sunset, and it seemed, over the miles and years beyond. He quietly spoke of his personal losses in the simplest and most poignant of terms.

"Everyone was gone..."

And now they are.

SOURCES

From *History of U.S. Marine Corps Operations in World War II*, Historical Branch, G-3 Division, Headquarters US Marine Corps.

(5 Volumes):

> Shaw, Jr., Henri I., Bernard, C. Nalty, and Edwin T. Turnbladh. Volume III. *Central Pacific Drive*. 1966.
>
> Garand, George W., and Truman R. Strobridge. Volume IV. *Western Pacific Operations*. 1971.

US Marines Historical Monographs, *Marines in World War II*. US Marine Corps Historical Section, Division of Public Information, Headquarters, US Marine Corps:

> Stockman, James R. 1947. *The Battle for Tarawa*.
>
> Heinl, Robert D., and John A. Crown. 1954. *The Marshalls: Increasing the Tempo*.
>
> Hoffman, Carl W. 1950. *Saipan: the Beginning of the End*.
>
> Hoffman, Carl W. 1951. *The Seizure of Tinian*.
>
> Barlety, Whitman S. 1954. *Iwo Jima: Amphibious Epic*.

From *Marines in World War II*, Commemorative Series, Marine Corps Historical Center, Washington, DC:

> Smith, Holland M., and Percy Flinch. 1989. *Coral and Brass*.
>
> Alexander, Joseph H. 1993. *Across the Reef: the Marine Assault of Tarawa*.
>
> Alexander, Joseph H. 1994. *Closing in: Marines in the Seizure of Iwo Jima*.

Chapin, John C. 1994. *Breaking the Outer Ring: Marine Landings in the Marshall Islands.*

Chapin, John C. 1994. *Breaching the Marianas: the Battle for Saipan.*

Harwood, Richard. 1994. *A Close Encounter: the Marine Landing on Tinian.*

Gayle, Gordon D. 1996. *Bloody Beaches: the Marines at Peleliu.*

The Fourth Marine Division in World War II, edited by Carl W. Proehl, from the private collection of Corporal William B. Allen.

Official operation reports of Regimental Combat Team Twenty-Three, Battalion Landing Team 3/23, and Battalion Landing Team 2/23 from Operations Flintlock, Forager, and Detachment (unclassified); from US National Archives, College Park, Maryland, and from the private collection of Steve McCloud, Trident Group, Chattanooga, Tennessee.

All World War II Pacific campaign photographic images of Roi-Namur, Saipan, and Iwo Jima are of official US Marine Corps photographs from the private collection of Steve McCloud, Trident Group, Chattanooga, Tennessee.

CPSIA information can be obtained at www.ICGtesting.com
Printed in the USA
LVOW12s2047260614

391878LV00028B/895/P